Environmental Invasion and Social Response

Of a Forest and Those Who Dwell Therein

SIL International®
Publications in Ethnography
48

The Publications in Ethnography series focuses on cultural studies of minority peoples of various parts of the world. While most volumes are authored by members of SIL International® who have done ethnographic research in a minority language, suitable works by others will also occasionally form part of the series.

Series Editor
Susan McQuay

Managing Editor
Eric Kindberg

Editorial Staff
Becky Quick, Volume Editor
Dawn Escoto, Proofreader
Gene Burnham, Proofreader

Production Staff
Lois Gourley, Production Director
Judy Benjamin, Compositor
Barbara Alber, Graphic Designer

Environmental Invasion and Social Response
Of a Forest and Those Who Dwell Therein

Douglas M. Fraiser

Foreword by Gerald F. Murray

SIL International®
Dallas, Texas

© 2019 by SIL International®
Library of Congress Catalog No: 2018966461
ISBN: 978-1-55671-395-8
ISSN: 0-0895-9897

Data and materials collected by researchers in an era before
documentation of permission was standardized may be
included in this publication. SIL makes diligent efforts to
identify and acknowledge sources and to obtain appropriate
permissions wherever possible, acting in good faith and on
the best information available at the time of publication.

Copies of this and other publications of SIL International®
may be obtained through distributors such as Amazon,
Barnes & Noble, other worldwide distributors and, for
select volumes, publications.sil.org:

SIL International Publications
7500 W. Camp Wisdom Road
Dallas, Texas 75236-5629 USA

General inquiry: publications_intl@sil.org
Pending order inquiry: sales@sil.org

Contents

Map and Figures

Tables

Foreword

Douglas Fraiser's work as an interdisciplinary ecologist emerges with descriptive clarity and analytic sophistication in this contribution to SIL International's growing series of volumes in the Publications in Ethnography series (his is listed as number 48). Though his PhD is in interdisciplinary ecology, his data-gathering methods and his theoretical analysis fall squarely within the evolving tradition of cultural anthropology.

The mountain-dwelling Manobo of the southern Philippines are a "non-Western" society, as were most of those studied by the earliest anthropologists. However, earlier researchers often approached their bands, tribes, and chiefdoms to document viable alternatives to Western culture, arguing for a relativistic, non-judgmental worldview. By the time Fraiser entered the field in the early 1980s, however, the non-judgmental relativism of earlier anthropology was on the wane (except perhaps in dealing with the alternative lifestyles that were springing up in the West). The new command drummed into fledgling anthropologists was to expose the multiple patterns of abuse, inequity, and oppression that humans have had the penchant for inflicting on each other throughout history and around the world. The Manobo studied by Fraiser were the targets of such powerful intruding forces.

There are three emergent themes that will ring bells to anthropologists who have worked elsewhere (in my case the Caribbean and Central America). The first is a replay in the Philippines of a sad drama that occurs in parallel fashion around the world. Indigenous mountain cultivators are now lodged within nation states. They continue to farm within mountain forests, but without formal title to the land. The State

suddenly defines their land as public land and gives concessions to logging companies and also admits non-indigenous landless settlers into
the region. The "slash and burn" swidden indigenous farming system
is declared to be environmentally harmful and agrarian tree cutting
is forbidden. The stated purpose: protect the environment. The real
purpose: protect the economic interests of logging companies, whose
clear-cutting tree removal does more environmental damage than any
indigenous ground-clearing procedures. The Manobo story is a replay
of similar patterns that I have personally observed in the Dominican
Republic and Honduras, but which are also documented around the
world. Fraiser also documents the problems. But his major emphasis
is the documentation of the energetic problem-solving response of the
Manobo to the intrusion of loggers and settlers.

That brings up a second theme that impresses the reader: Fraiser's ability to go beyond description of the Manobo response and to enter into a
theoretically sensitive analysis of the causal factors—economic and demographic—that engendered the crisis and that subsequently triggered off
and shaped this social-structural response. The Manobo have invented an
organizational "tool" (in Fraiser's words) to resist and deal with loggers,
settlers, and the State. The description of the crisis and the response is by
itself interesting: loggers and settlers threaten, and the Manobo respond
with a religious movement which blossomed into 114 centers that effectively moves the State to curb outside intrusions. Fraiser's causal analysis of
this process, however, adds additional theoretical depth to the fascinating
descriptive account.

The role of religion as a mechanism of resistance raises yet a third
issue that rings bells around the world. Most Western academics have
gone beyond a simplistic essentialist view of religion as an "opiate of the
masses," as an ideological mechanism of oppression. Several early anthropologists and sociologists held a countervailing irenic view of religion as
a positive mechanism of social stability. Among the Manobo, religion was
mobilized neither as a tool of oppression nor as a tool of internal harmony.
The adopted religion—a generic version of Protestant Christianity—has
functioned instead as a mechanism of resistance to outside loggers and
settlers.

The facts that Fraiser presents in this particular case, however, may generate intellectual malaise among a subset of anthropologists and other academics whose knee-jerk reaction to Protestant missionaries is to critique
them as agents of "ethnocide" intent on destroying traditional culture.
A common anthropological theme song is "Indigenous religion, hooray,
Christianity, boo." (The choir curiously seems less indignant, or at least a
bit more silent, about the spread of Islam.) The Manobo in contrast have
harnessed Christianity as a mechanism of resistance—non-violent but
effective—against logging companies and settlers. They have imbued their

Christianity with the pragmatic this-worldly orientation that characterized their traditional religion. Fraiser puts it well:

> The accounts given by my informants indicate that pastors were involved in addressing land rights from the very beginning.... They preached, prayed for the sick, settled disputes, and led their people in dealing with conflicts with the settlers and loggers. When the Manobo converted to Christianity, it appears that they ... considered it appropriate for their new spiritual leaders to be concerned about matters of this world as well as the next. (p. 76)

Fraiser makes the interesting observation that the emergence of a resistance element in Manobo Protestantism was neither spearheaded nor even anticipated by the foreign SIL personnel, who focused on linguistic issues affecting Bible translation. The Manobo pastors themselves initiated the resistance movement. Fraiser also points out religious parallels in the Western hemisphere. The US Civil Rights movement of the 1960s was spearheaded by Rev. Martin Luther King Jr. and Black leaders still often bear the title "Reverend." He also cites the liberation theology of Latin American Catholicism as another example of religiously formulated resistance. (Its frequent linkage to Marxist calls for violence, however, inject a theme that is not found in Manobo Protestantism, which emphasizes organized legal maneuvers.)

Fraiser is not positing any inherent tendency in Protestantism to become involved in land tenure or logging conflicts. He points out that had the Catholic Church initiated literacy campaigns and organized communities, the Manobo would probably have adopted Catholicism. The country Haiti, where I have worked at length, illustrates well this Catholic/Protestant game of musical chairs. Under the Duvalier dictatorship, Protestant missionaries provided health care and educational services but avoided any involvement with politics or any organized protest against economic or social grievances. The Catholic Church, in contrast, played a major role in the overthrow of Duvalier. The Catholic radio station was a thorn in the side of the regime. Catholic priests, many of them Belgian, French, and American missionaries, were organizing small agrarian solidarity groups in the rural areas to protect farmers against abuse from local civilian militia agents. During his visit in the 1980s, Pope John Paul II infuriated the government by his call for radical change in Haiti. After Duvalier fled in 1986, the largest slum in Port-au-Prince, which had been named after Duvalier's mother, was renamed after the Catholic radio station, and a major street was given the name of John Paul II. A radical Catholic priest (by then an ex-priest) was eventually elected president with an overwhelming majority. The contrast is interesting. In the Haitian context, it was the Catholic Church that organized resistance. Among the Philippine Manobo, the thorn in the side of settlers, loggers, and the State has been a network of 114 recently formed Protestant churches, created by the Manobo themselves.

One anthropological lesson to be derived from this is that the basic internal elements of a religious system—its theology, its rituals, its leadership structures, its scriptures—can remain stable. But its external functions—political, economic, environmental, educational, medical, etc.—can evolve and vary from place to place and from time to time under the causal impact of economic, social, and political dynamics exogenous to the theology and rituals of the religious system itself. In this sense, Douglas Fraiser is to be congratulated for providing us with insights, not only into the specific ethnography of the Philippine Manobo, but also into the more general causal factors that can potentially drive the functional evolution of religious systems.

Gerald F. Murray, PhD
Visiting Professor, School of Law and Political Sciences,
    Shanghai Normal University
Retired (emeritus) from the Department of Anthropology,
    University of Florida

Preface

When my wife, Meg, and I went to work with the Manobo people in 1983, we had no idea how great a part of our lives they would become. We had been preparing for careers in community development and had just finished masters' degrees at the University of Florida. Meg's degree was in Food Science and Human Nutrition, mine in Agronomy. Using a computerized job matching service, we learned about a small Christian mission in the Philippines that was working with the Manobo and were looking for someone who could help them in economic development. We applied and were accepted, and in November we left for the Philippines. We expected to be there three years.

We left the Manobo in 1986, sure we would never live with them again, and only see them on rare visits. We applied to SIL International and were accepted. To our surprise, they asked us to return to the Philippines and continue working with the Manobo. In 1989 we went back with our first-born son, Ian. Our second son, Kirk, was born in Mindanao two years later, in 1991. We finally completed our work with the Manobo in 2002, at which time we left the Philippines.

Again, though, our life with the Manobo was not over. SIL asked us to become consultants in community development and anthropology, and to better prepare for that role, I entered a doctoral program at the University of Florida in 2003. I decided to major in interdisciplinary ecology, as it would allow me to concentrate on anthropology while incorporating concepts from ecology and agricultural economics. My advisor in the anthropology department, Dr. Gerald Murray, suggested that I conduct my research on the Manobo, as I already knew the language, had years of observations, and had an extensive network of contacts among them.[1]

This book is the result of that study. The people, places, and events in it are entirely real. Note, though, that I have used pseudonyms in cases where people might be endangered if their identities were known.

The Cotabato Manobo (whom I will refer to hereafter as "Manobo") are horticulturalists living in the highlands of the southern Philippines. While they live in a small part of the Philippines, their situation is similar to that being acted out many places on this planet. Largely isolated from mainstream Philippine society until the middle of last century, their territory is now flooded with newcomers. The government considers their land to be national forest and has opened it up for logging and settlement. Existence for the Manobo has never been easy, but the new pressures generated by the state, logging company, and settlers make it much harder. There are not only the direct effects of violence and loss of land and food, but many indirect effects occur as well. They have been forced off the better soils onto marginal land, making farming more difficult and encouraging environmental degradation.

However, not all pressures are material. The low regard of many newcomers for the Manobo has inspired a search for respect and significance, one result of which has been a great interest in literacy for both adults and children. And awareness of more prosperous lifestyles has resulted in considerable interest in new agricultural techniques and in health care. In other words, the Manobo have not passively accepted their situation but are actively seeking to deal with it. As they do so, they are relying upon one of their most significant tools, social organization.

The study of "tools" usually implies a focus on "technology," by which we mean physical implements. This is an unfortunately narrow focus. When people have problems, they deal with them through the use of means—tools—which can be either material or nonmaterial. This concept of social organization as a problem-solving tool brings to mind a stroll I took through the back alleys of Rome on the way from one famous ruin to another. On

---

[1] The Cotabato Manobo language has been given the ISO 639-3 identifier of "mta" by the International Organization for Standardization (Lewis et al. 2015a). The Cotabato Manobo people call themselves *Menubù*. However, this form is not found in the literature, the Hispanicized forms of Manobo and Manuvù being used instead. As there are some twenty Manobo languages, local place names were used to distinguish between them. The modifier "Cotabato" came from the province in which the Cotabato Manobo lived. That province has since been divided, with the result that a city far from the Cotabato Manobo is now called Cotabato, while the Cotabato Manobo live nowhere near it. Some of the Cotabato Manobo have taken to calling themselves Dulangan Manobo, after one of their ancestors, and that designation is now common in much of their interaction with the Philippine government, though is not common in the academic literature. For purposes of convenience, I will henceforth refer to the group simply as the "Manobo."

one path, fifty or more stray cats had temporarily made an alley their home. Some human authority would one day decide the cats would have to leave, and they would be at the mercy of the powers-that-be. But unlike feline populations, humans can, and often do, respond to outside intrusions, not only with physical implements but also with new social-organizational arrangements to respond to the unwanted interventions of outside forces, such as the loggers and settlers invading Manobo territory. Humans are at liberty to respond like cats and simply dissolve and scatter. But they are also at liberty to reorganize and retrench, as the Manobo have begun doing.

As the invasions of their territory and their consequences are beyond the ability of a single household to deal with, the Manobo are using social structures for supradomestic cooperation. However, like physical implements, social structures may serve more than one purpose. And just as societies develop new physical implements for new tasks, societies may also develop new social structures to meet new needs, or use an old structure in a new way. I began my research with the working hypothesis that the structures the Manobo were using to respond to outside forces were derived in part from the Manobo's traditional social structure, but that the Manobo may have modified these time-proven tools for new tasks. I therefore set out to document the Manobo's traditional and emerging cultural tools for cooperation, to elucidate the processes by which new organizational forms have emerged, and to relate the characteristics of those traditional and emerging forms to their effectiveness in attaining group goals. In the process, I also hoped to anticipate whether the Manobo's ultimate response to the invasion of their homeland would mirror that of the scattered Roman cats, or reflect the many other human populations who have responded organizationally to new challenges.

Indigenous groups around the world have developed a variety of responses to outside forces, some more effective than others. My research with the Manobo is a case study of the drama being played out worldwide as indigenous societies utilize their traditional cultures—and modify them—to respond to changes brought on by their governments and by other forces their governments have permitted and encouraged. My intent has been that this work not only be theoretically rigorous but also eminently practical. It is written for those working directly with local communities, whether they be in government, non-governmental organizations, or peoples' organizations. Such field workers often begin their work in seemingly non-political areas important to the local community (such as literacy, health, agricultural development). Because of concern for the community, they later become involved in land issues. As we will see, these areas are often far more closely intertwined than we usually realize. My hope is that what I have written here will provide greater theoretical insight into the relationships and processes involved and thereby, in some measure, contribute to the well-being of indigenous peoples worldwide.

Organization, terminology, and abbreviations

Chapter 1 provides a brief introduction to this study, giving a sketch of the setting, the questions I was interested in answering, and the process of study. The theoretical approaches used are covered in chapter 2. Chapters 3 through 6 detail one instance of a drama that is being played out in countless places around the world: the intrusion of a dominant society into indigenous territory and the consequent response of the indigenous population. The case of the Cotabato Manobo people is, of course, of intense interest to themselves and to those who live near them. But it is also of interest to other indigenous communities and to those who interact with them, for it elucidates the specific processes involved in the interaction of traditional society with the world thrust upon them. Chapters 3 and 4 cover the early years of the Manobo's history, during which time the Manobo were largely at the mercy of outside forces. In chapter 5, I bring out the development of civil associations and the foundation they formed for political resistance (that is, the active pursuit of land rights and personal security through cooperative action). Chapter 6 traces the emergence of political resistance from the earlier civil associations. In chapter 7 we pause to examine those civil associations, to elucidate the factors affecting cooperation in political resistance. Chapter 8 completes our examination of the Manobo's response to the invasion of their territory, while chapter 9 summarizes my findings and makes recommendations to each of the stakeholders involved. Chapter 10, the Epilogue, is a brief update on the current situation.

A few brief notes on terminology will be helpful to readers unfamiliar with the Philippines. The country's political divisions, from largest to smallest, are regions, provinces, municipalities, *barangay* (also called barrios), and *sitios*. Provinces are headed by a governor, municipalities by a mayor, and *barangay* (barrios) by a *barangay* captain (barrio captain). Regions have no governing officer over them; they are used mainly to provide a level intermediate between the national and provincial offices for government agencies (for example, DENR and NCIP). In US terms, provinces are equivalent to states, municipalities to counties, *barangay* to districts or towns, and *sitios* to precincts.

The linguistic and ethnic makeup of the Philippines is complex, with the country having at least 182 distinct languages (Lewis et al. 2015b) and a variety of religions, with language and religion frequently not correlated. Consequently, standard English does not contain universally understood cover terms for the groups I discuss in this book. The majority of the Filipinos who have settled in Manobo territory are from Philippine peoples who were heavily influenced by the Spanish: Visayans from the central islands of the Philippines, and Tagalogs and Ilocanos from Luzon. I will refer to these people as "settlers." However, a number of people from the Maguindanao and other heavily Muslim groups have also settled in Manobo territory. As they consider themselves culturally distinct from the other settlers, I will refer to these people as "Muslim," even though this confuses religion with ethnicity and not all adhere to the teachings of Islam.

I have used abbreviations for some organizations and legal arrangements that I frequently refer to. For ease of reference, those abbreviations are listed below, as well as when used in the text.

Acknowledgements

The story behind this book belongs to the Manobo and Tiruray, the mountain peoples of the Philippines with whom I lived. But there are many others who have been a part of my efforts to understand their story and to share it with others. My thanks go to all of them.

Key among these is Dr. Gerald Murray, the chair of my doctoral advisory committee. His knowledge of theory, experience with the practical application of anthropology, and insistence on clear thinking have been invaluable in my growth as a researcher and field worker. His wisdom, patience, and commitment to apprenticing me over the four years of my study were a tremendous encouragement.

I am grateful for the insights and suggestions of my advisory committee members, Dr. Michael Bannister, Dr. Abraham Goldman, Dr. Peter Hildebrand, and Dr. Marianne Schmink. Particular thanks go to Dr. Schmink for her encouragement to consider graduate studies.

My research would have never begun were it not for Ms. Joanne Shetler, SIL colleague who worked with the Balangao people in the northern Philippines; she encouraged my interest in anthropology and mentored my early efforts. I am thankful to Dr. Sherwood Lingenfelter, who led the workshop on social organization that showed me the practical application of anthropology. Dr. Thomas Headland, SIL colleague who has worked with the Casiguran Agta of the northern Philippines, has been invaluable as a mentor, both during my studies and in my subsequent work. The words and thoughts in this book are my own, and I take sole responsibility for them, but their expression has benefited greatly from his thoughtful review and suggestions. Thank you, Tom.

My studies would hardly have been possible without substantial financial assistance. I owe special thanks to the School of Natural Resources and Environment and the Graduate School of the University of Florida for an E. T. York Presidential Fellowship and assistantship that made this study possible, and to Dr. Raymond Gallaher for encouraging me to apply. My thanks go also to the University's Working Forests in the Tropics Program for a summer research grant, supported by the National Science Foundation (DGE-0221599); to SIL International and SIL Philippines for assistance with both educational and research expenses; and to the many individuals who supported my work with the Manobo and who continued to support me during my studies.

My special thanks go to the Manobo and Tiruray among whom I have lived and worked. Their care and friendship over many years, and their willingness to have my wife and me labor alongside them, made it a joy to live among them. My only regret is that changes in the documentation required to establish permission to use an individual's name have changed since I conducted my research; inability to obtain some informants' signatures at this time has made it necessary to use pseudonyms for them.

Finally, I am grateful to my sons, Ian and Kirk, for their cheerful appreciation of the special life they have had growing up among the Manobo, and to Meg, my wife, friend, and co-laborer, for her love, support, and commitment to me and the work to which we have been called. Her presence with me has made this journey immeasurably lighter and brighter.

Abbreviations

AMBCI	Association of Manobo Bible Churches, Inc.
ATBCI	Association of Téduray Bible Churches, Inc.
CADC	Certificate of Ancestral Domain Claim
CADT	Certificate of Ancestral Domain Title (successor to the CADC)
CPR	common property regime, common property resource, common-pool resource
DENR	Department of Environment and Natural Resources, the national governmental agency charged with oversight of natural resources
IPRA	Indigenous Peoples Rights Act
M&S Co.	Magsaysay and Sons logging company
NCIP	National Commission on Indigenous Peoples
NGO	nongovernmental organization
PAFID	Philippine Agency for Intercultural Development
PO	people's organization
SIL	SIL International
TAP	Translators Association of the Philippines
TCEA	Tribal Community of Esperanza Association
TCLA	Tribal Community of Lebak Association

Map 1. The Philippines

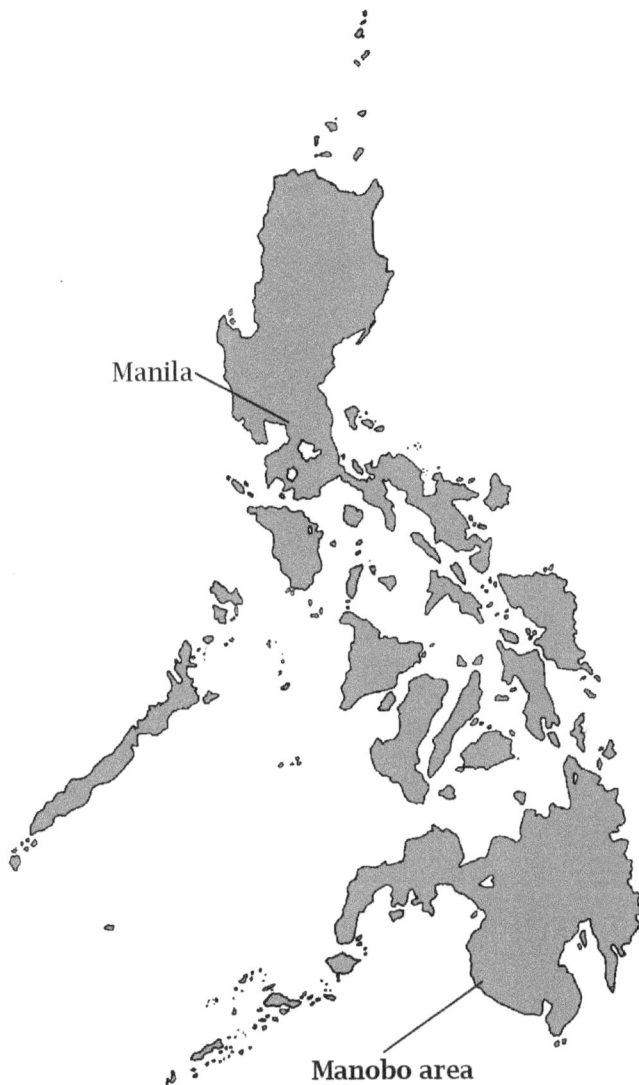

Manila

Manobo area

1

A Trip to the Toolshed:
Theoretical Foundations

Before considering how the Manobo have used their culture to respond
to the invasions of their homeland, and how they modified their culture
to do so, it will be helpful to go over the theoretical approaches I used as
I sought to understand their experience. We will begin with the areas of
social organization and cooperation. We will then shift our focus to the
arena where the Manobo are desperately applying the tools of social organization, namely, conflicts over land and other natural resources. Finally, we
will conclude with a brief survey of the literature on insular Southeast Asian
societies for features that contribute to understanding how the Manobo use
social structures for supradomestic cooperation.

Theories of social organization: Description

Two of the greatest questions concerning social organization are 1) how
to describe it and 2) what the cause-and-effect relationships are between
a people's culture and their environment—by which I mean not only flora
and fauna and water and soil, but also the pressures brought to bear by
exogenous groups and societies. We will consider the issue of description
first.

The ethnographic approach

Anthropology originally took a holistic approach to the description of culture. Its goal was ethnography—the description of every aspect of a people's culture, including their means of subsistence, technology and artifacts, religious beliefs and practices, life cycles, and family and community structures. Over time, the focus has shifted toward particular cultural domains and specific issues, and anthropology has developed new and useful frameworks for that purpose. The new frameworks, though, rest on the basic concepts of social organization employed in the ethnographic approach, so a brief review of them is in order.

The basic components of social organization, described well by Murdock (1965) and Keesing (1975) and in texts such as that by Spradley and McCurdy (1980), focus on the articulation of groups and individuals, and include the concepts of status, rank, and role. More recent work on household and community economics (Small and Tannenbaum 1999a, 1999b) suggests a focus on the interactions between individual and household, household and community, and community and outside world. This provides useful units of analysis, with the caveat that the "community" is itself a complex network comprised of numerous interlocked interest and kinship groups.

Economic anthropology—the study of the relationships between social structure and the production and transfer of resources—elaborates on the traditional approach. Firth (1951:125) concurs with most economists that "The basic concept of economics is the allocation of scarce, available resources between realizable human wants, with the recognition that alternatives are possible in each sphere." However, he goes on to observe that social relationships generally have an economic aspect, even when no "price" is involved, in that they involve choices made regarding time and energy (Firth 1951:130). Individuals may work not only for monetary remuneration but also to satisfy social expectations to ensure they retain the benefits of membership in their social group (Firth 1951:141–142). In non-monetary economies (or relationships dominated by social rather than monetary concerns), production may be specified by norms (Firth 1951:133). Further, there is often considerable direct matching of goods and services, based on normative comparisons of their relative worth. There also tends to be far less separation of the roles common in modern industrial societies: capitalist, entrepreneur, workman, and manager. Participants in an enterprise may fill multiple roles, and production may be only one facet of a social relationship (Firth 1951:136).

Social network analysis

One approach to social relationships has capitalized on the fact that social relationships, like any other system, can be represented visually. This approach has led to social network analysis, which focuses on the geometric qualities of the network. These include attributes such as how many members each individual in the network is connected to, and whether the network looks like a net or like a branching tree. John Scott's (2000) *Social Network Analysis* is an excellent treatise on the theory and practice of social network analysis.

One important feature of many social networks is the presence of "structural holes" (Burt 2002). When each member of a group is connected to all the other members near him, the group is tightly bound together, but information must pass through a large number of individuals to make its way through the network. If the network is fragmented into several smaller tight clusters with only occasional links between them, information takes even longer to travel. However, the creation of bridges between unconnected clusters greatly reduces the distance that information must travel. Krebs (n.d.) brings out that this results in the information traveling more quickly and with less distortion. Thus, network structure can have a profound effect on how quickly and appropriately a group can respond to threats.

Another important concept is that of strong and weak links (Granovetter 1973). Links between members of tight groups are often strong, in that they are multiplex and charged with affect. Bridging links between clusters are often weak, as between acquaintances rather than close friends. However, it is these weak links that provide individuals with knowledge they do not normally possess because they already know much of what their closest associates do. In the same way, village-level networks will likely be strong, while the weak links of acquaintance formed during occasional conferences with other Philippine indigenous peoples or NGOs may provide the foundation for weaker but still effective networks at the regional or national level (see chapter 5, footnote 6).

Social capital

Another approach to interpersonal relationships is to consider the material benefit they bring to the individuals who have them. Viewed in this way, relationships can be considered "social capital." While the social capital theory owes its origins to several writers, perhaps the name most closely associated with it is that of Robert Putnam. Putnam (1993:15–16) was impressed with the differences in governmental styles and outcomes in the north and south of Italy. He attributed the differences to historical events nearly a thousand years before, when a powerful monarchy was established in southern Italy, versus a cluster of "communal republics" in the north. In his view, the vertical relationships typical of the monarchy and the horizontal relationships typical of the republics set up social patterns which have continued to the present. Putnam concluded that the more "civic" the society—that is, the greater the incidence of horizontal, non-governmental

relationships between individuals—the more effectively the society functioned. Putnam later applied the term "social capital" to such horizontal,
non-governmental linkages.

The concept has found ready acceptance with the World Bank and other
financial development institutions. In the World Bank's (2002a) analysis,
civil society is contrasted with both government and market, and horizontal relationships within civil society produce another "estate" that allows
for power being brought against the state, if need be. This appears to be
what has taken place in the Manobo's efforts to obtain land rights. They
had attempted to drive settlers (as defined in the preface) out of one portion
of their ancestral territory in the early 1970s but were quickly overcome
by the military. Military defeat, coupled with the government's establishment of its own administrative structure as legally superior to local leaders,
greatly weakened the traditional political structure.

Confronted with these outside forces, the Manobo did what many other
peoples have done in similar situations: they utilized religious structures
and symbols to respond to disparities in power. But while the famous
parallel instances of the Ghost Dance of Native Americans and the cargo
cults of Melanesia (Kapferer 1997) employed traditional religious symbols,
the Christianized Manobo, as is true of Brazilian and Guatemalan adherents
of Liberation Theology, have utilized an indigenized form of Christianity
to mobilize new organizational forces.[1] Their adaptation of Christianity has
its roots in the vernacular literacy program that SIL began in the 1950s.
A portion of the literacy material consisted of Judeo-Christian texts,
translated into Manobo. Much as the Kiowa and Sioux responded to an
outside religious form (Kracht 1992), an increasing number of Manobo
responded to the Biblical texts. The result was the emergence of churches
under indigenous leadership and using the vernacular through much of
Manobo territory. At the same time, SIL's pursuit of vernacular literacy
resulted in an expanding cadre of Manobo literacy teachers.

The result may have been surprising to SIL. The Manobo took a pacifist
interpretation of Christianity, and the internecine violence that had been
so common diminished remarkably. With a new freedom to travel within
their own territory, church and literacy leaders began meeting together at
frequent intervals, thereby forming a network of relationships throughout
the language group. At the same time, the church leaders began to represent
their congregants in much the same way as the traditional *datù* had. Unlike
the *datù*, though, whose travel had been restricted by Manobo-on-Manobo

---

[1] Contrary to its frequent dismissal as "the opiate of the masses," religion has
played a significant part in mobilizing resistance in many well-known political
movements, including the African-American civil rights movement (Rev. Dr. Martin
Luther King Jr., Rev. Al Sharpton, and Rev. Jesse Jackson), Mohandas Gandhi's
struggle for Indian independence, and contemporary Sunni and Shiite movements
in the Middle East.

violence, the church leaders freely associated with pastors from throughout the language group. They developed a network of relationships that surpassed anything the Manobo had ever had.

As has happened in other settings, the local religious leaders went beyond purely "spiritual" matters to mobilize social resistance. In the mid-1990s, the leaders of the church association formally petitioned the government for the formation of a Manobo reservation. Since the government has been slow in responding to that request the Manobo have had to form other organizations devoted solely to the pursuit of land rights. It is apparent, though, in terms of the social capital paradigm, that it was the mobilization of links in the civil realm (of which religious groups form a subset) that enabled the Manobo to mobilize for the pursuit of rights to their ancestral lands. Several church and literacy leaders continue to be instrumental in that effort.

Proponents of social capital have not been unaware of the existence of vertical relationships. Putnam (1993:178–179), for instance, observed that in "prisoner's dilemma" situations, people may either defect or reciprocate help, and that these become social norms. He goes on to write that "reciprocity/trust and dependence/exploitation can each hold society together, though at quite different levels of efficiency and institutional performance." Reciprocal relationships are horizontal, while relationships of dominance and dependence are vertical. Yet, despite acknowledging the presence of vertical relationships, Putnam goes on to focus almost exclusively on the presence or absence of "social capital" (horizontal relationships), thus leaving the role of vertical relationships outside the scope of his theory.

While proponents of social capital theory are enthusiastic about the benefits of social capital to a society, they have noted that there can be drawbacks as well. The World Bank (2002a), for instance, notes that while individuals may benefit from their ties to particular groups, group demands on the individual may sometimes outweigh benefits. The World Bank (2002b) also notes that groups may exclude others from their benefits or act exploitatively against those outside the group. The close relationship that seems to exist between certain government offices and companies that want to extract lumber and minerals from the Manobo's territory is a good example. The World Bank (2002c) likewise notes that while social capital can reduce a firm's (or other group's) transaction costs and give it a competitive edge, such close ties can also result in nepotism or abusive monopoly.

These drawbacks to social capital bring out a problem with the theory— namely, its failure to account for negative human relationships. "Capital" as a financial term is considered an asset and is not used to refer to liabilities. Social capital theorists likewise speak of the presence or absence of social capital, but fail to acknowledge the presence of actively harmful relationships. Writers such as Harriss (2001:12) and Fine (2000:199) have criticized proponents of social capital theory for deliberately covering up the presence of exploitation and the consequent necessity for political action. However, the difficulty may be due simply to trying to use financial terminology that is not equipped to contain all of the realities of human interactions.

The theory also suffers from serious problems of aggregation in measuring social capital (Fine 2000:176–178). The typical approach to social capital relies on indicators such as generalized trust, membership in organizations, and norms such as reciprocity, cooperation, and tolerance (Adam and Rončević 2003). Such a generalized view of society can readily overlook the existence of tight clusters that exclude or exploit others in society, as well as clusters that are shut out of the power structure. This is a serious error, but is probably better charged to the account of proponents of the theory than to the theory itself. A similar error of aggregation is often made in addressing national measures of wealth. The traditional approach simply adds the money owned by each member of society without any consideration of the networking of productive assets (for example, whether sources of coal and iron ore are connected to smelting plants and then to automobile factories through roads, railroads, and canals). This does not render the concept of economic capital useless. It merely indicates that when attributes are considered at the level of an entire society (or even a neighborhood), aggregation is methodologically inadequate.

There are several problems with the social capital concept. Its exclusive focus on horizontal relationships, its accounting of only the presence or absence of good relationships, and problems with aggregation have all tended to lead practitioners to overlook the negative effect of groups that exclude or exploit the rest of society. However, social capital theory provides a service in pointing out that social relationships are not only social, but also enable individuals and groups to attain many non-social benefits. The Manobo's social relationships have served them as invaluable "capital," allowing them to band together to seek land rights and to operate literacy and health programs.

Grid-group theory

The theory of social capital has been criticized for overlooking differences in power in social relationships. The same criticism might be leveled against social network analysis as it tends to represent all relationships as being essentially horizontal. While neither approach specifies that relationships are between equals, neither method requires the researcher to distinguish between peer and non-peer relationships, nor provides a ready means of handling non-peer relationships. In contrast, grid-group theory (also known as culture theory) explicitly recognizes that relationships are either between equals (horizontal) or non-equals (vertical). Mary Douglas, the originator of the theory (1970), suggested that much of

> [t]he variability of an individual's involvement in social life can be...captured by two dimensions of sociality: group and grid. *Group* refers to the extent to which an individual is incorporated into bounded units. The greater the incorporation, the more individual choice is subject to group determination. *Grid* denotes the degree to which an individual's life is circumscribed by externally imposed prescriptions. The more binding and extensive the scope of the prescriptions, the less of life that is open to individual negotiation. (Thompson et al. 1980:5)

Essentially, "group" describes the constraints and opportunities incumbent upon an individual due to horizontal relationships, while "grid" does the same for vertical relationships.

The existence of vertical and horizontal relationships is hardly a new discovery. Putnam (1993:178–179), for instance, noted that "reciprocity/ trust and dependence/exploitation can each hold society together, though at quite different levels of efficiency and institutional performance." Douglas' contribution was in recognizing that these two aspects of relationships describe a large portion of social interaction and of people's belief systems. She used the terms "cultural bias," "social relations," and "way of life" to describe the relationship between them. Cultural bias designated "shared values and beliefs," while social relations designated "patterns of interpersonal relations" (Thompson et al. 1980:1), making the two terms equivalent to "worldview" and "social organization," respectively. A viable combination of the two is referred to as a way of life.

The combination of presence or absence of these two kinds of relationships—horizontal or vertical—gives rise to a typology of four types of societies (Thompson et al. 1980:1–10): a society (or group) that is low group and low grid is Individualist; one that is high group and low grid is Egalitarian; high group and high grid characterize a Hierarchical society; while low group and high grid specify a Fatalistic society.[2]

Grid-group theory recognizes that social control is a matter of power. As Thompson et al. (1980:6–7) state it:

> In the grid-group framework individuals are manipulated and try to manipulate others. It is the form of power—who is or is not entitled to exercise power over others—that differs. ...Strong group boundaries coupled with minimal prescriptions produce social relations that are *Egalitarian*. ...When an individual's social environment is characterized by strong group boundaries and binding prescriptions,

---

[2] Singelis et al. (1995) use different terminology but propose essentially the same typology. Instead of low and high group, they speak of collectivist and individualist orientation; instead of low and high grid, they use horizontal and vertical orientation.

the resulting social relations are *Hierarchical*...Individuals who are bound by neither group incorporation nor prescribed roles inhabit an *Individualistic* social context. ...Although the individualist is, by definition, relatively free from control by others, that does not mean the person is not engaged in exerting control over others. On the contrary, the individualist's success is often measured by the size of the following the person can command. People who find themselves subject to binding prescriptions and are excluded from group membership exemplify the *Fatalistic* way of life.

Some have objected that a classification of all societies into just four types is rather limiting, but Thompson et al. (1980:3–4) point out that the two-times-two typology "more than doubles the amount of conceptual variety available in existing theories of social organization...Whatever their singular merits may be, and these are considerable, the great social theorists of the past rarely went beyond the development from hierarchy to individualism, thereby leaving out fatalism, egalitarianism, and autonomy."

Grid-group analysis reveals "how various arguments in families, churches, political parties, and sports clubs involve the fundamental issues of where the institution should draw its group boundary, and how it should regulate itself internally" (Gross and Rayner 1985:18).

One of the most promising contributions of grid-group theory is its notion of how the four ways of life are not only in competition but also interdependent, as this helps reveal the process by which alliances between apparently incompatible patterns of social organization may arise. Thompson et al. (1980:4) observe that "Each way of life needs each of its rivals, either to make up for its deficiencies, or to exploit, or to define itself against." They describe the alliances that can form between each of the ways of life (1980:83–99). Alliance of individualism with hierarchism produces what we call "the establishment." Individualists gain the protection of property rights, while hierarchists benefit from the enhanced economic growth arising from the activity of individualist entrepreneurs. Egalitarians often avoid alliances with either individualists or hierarchists, preferring to maintain a firm boundary between their collective way of life and the outside world. However, they may seek alliance with another way of life if they wish to influence events in the outside world. Alliance may be sought with hierarchists by appealing to the hierarchists' values that those at the top have an obligation to help those below them, and that individuals should be willing to sacrifice for the entire society. Fatalists are typically resigned so seldom attempt to influence events. However, they provide benefits to each of the other ways of life. To egalitarians, fatalists provide moral ammunition with which to attack the establishment, and their position as powerless and exploited makes them attractive to egalitarians as ready recruits to their cause. Individualists, who aspire to maintain their freedom while asserting control over others, value fatalists as the necessary "servants" within their networks. Hierarchists may fault the fatalists for their lack of support for the system, but value having a complacent mass that will not challenge the decisions of established leaders.

Prior observation suggests that the Manobo usually act within the individualist and egalitarian ways of life, Philippine authorities act as in-charge individualists or hierarchists, and representatives of NGOs act as egalitarians or hierarchists. Grid-group theory may therefore shed light on the interactions between the different groups.

Theories of social organization: Culture change

Having considered several ways of describing social organization, we now turn to causal relationships between social organization and a society's sociophysical environment. As such relationships are more readily apparent when a society is undergoing change, the discipline that reveals the most about such relationships is that of culture change. One of the most prominent theories of culture change is that of cultural evolution.

Cultural evolution

Anthropological theories since the mid-nineteenth century have focused heavily on causal relationships between culture and the material world. Perhaps the school that has concentrated most on this issue is that of cultural evolution. Theories of cultural evolution therefore help to identify major factors in the sociophysical environment that influence social organization and that are affected by social organization.

Typologies

Cultural evolution has often assumed that societies progress from simple to complex (Rambo 1991b), but this is not an essential part of the theory. Richard Adams (1977), for instance, describes situations in which one society becomes less complex as a result of unsuccessful competition with a more powerful society. While cultural evolution does not necessitate adherence to a unilineal view of history, the search for patterns of how societies respond in cause-and-effect fashion to various forces does predispose the theory toward the development of typologies. The most widely used typologies have been based on technology, means of subsistence, and forms of social–political organization (Rambo 1991b). Technology provided the basis for Lewis Henry Morgan's classification system, but it showed a poor fit with cultural characteristics. In contrast, taxonomies based on means of subsistence are widely used. Hunter-gatherer, swidden[3] farmer, and pastoralist are commonly used categories. However, while means of

---

[3] Swidden farming is also referred to as "shifting cultivation" and "slash-and-burn."

subsistence is undoubtedly important, there is not a one-to-one relationship between means of subsistence and other aspects of culture. As Rambo points out, the Northwest Coast Native Americans are a classic case of disjunction between theory and reality. Their economy was based on hunting and gathering, but was socially complex, with stratification usually associated with a highly developed form of agriculture. Furthermore, many societies rely upon a mix of subsistence strategies (Hutterer 1991).

Another well-known typology is Elman Service's (Yengoyan 1991) categorization of societies as bands, tribes, chiefdoms, kingdoms, and states. He later consolidated these categories into the egalitarian society, the hierarchical society, and the archaic civilization or classical empire. While Yengoyan (1991) considered this a less useful classification system, it remains in use (for example, Rambo 1991a; Rambo 1991b; Service 1993). Morton Fried proposed a similar taxonomy, progressing from egalitarian society to rank society to stratified society to state (Rambo 1991b). Fried (1975:i) objected to the term "tribe" on the ground that "tribes, as conventionally conceived, are not closely bounded populations in either territorial or demographic senses. They are not economically and politically integrated and display political organization under hierarchical leaders only as a result of contact with already existing states." While his comments suggest caution in applying these typologies carelessly, the point remains that they can be useful for comparing and understanding societies. Each of these typologies differentiates between societies on the basis of how they exercise social control over their members and the extent to which individuals can exercise control over resources and other people (Rambo 1991b).

The Manobo, prior to extensive contact with mainstream Philippine society, appear to have fit Service's tribe category. Their situation is now more complex. Having been incorporated closely into the Philippine state, they are hardly a stereotypical tribe. As Fried suggested, their initial move toward greater organization was stimulated by outside forces. Their continued efforts to organize for a variety of purposes have resulted in a more complex organization, a process which continues. Nevertheless, while they do not neatly fit the ideal of any single category, description of their organization (and that of other groups they have relations with) is made much easier by the use a widely understood classification system.

Factors shaping culture

Energy, power, and money

Perhaps the most-asked question among adherents of cultural evolution is what factors most govern culture. Several possibilities have been put forward, including energy, technology, carrying capacity of the environment, and population level. Richard Adams (1988:xiv–xv), in an effort to bring the physical and social sciences onto common ground, has suggested that energy is the one concept common to both. He proposes viewing social interactions in terms of thermodynamics (Adams 1975:109), suggesting that social organization arises from the energy relations between persons in a fashion parallel to how the physical structure of water in soil depends on the temperature, atmospheric pressure, and matric suction at a particular location in the soil.

Other writers have focused on the ability of a society to capture energy. What has become known as White's Law states, "Culture evolves as the amount of energy harnessed per capita per year is increased, or the efficiency of the instrumental means of putting the energy to work is increased" (Rambo 1991a:5). Rambo agrees with White that the total use of energy increases with social complexity, but found that per capita usage drops in the progression from band to tribe to chiefdom, and then increases tremendously in movement to industrial society. Rachman's (1991) comparison of a band in Indonesia with a tribal society in Malaysia confirms Rambo's observations. The tribal society consumed less energy per capita but more energy in total, and spent a higher percentage and quantity of energy on social activities such as visiting and entertainment. Rambo (1991a:303) identifies the mechanisms for social integration as the consumer of this energy. In his words, as societies "become more specialized and have to embrace a larger number and greater diversity of components, the means of integration demand an ever larger quantity of energy. Rather than being used to achieve individual goals, a growing share of available energy is used to support the functioning of the system." Taken together, the literature indicates that as societies become more complex, they use more energy in total, and expend a greater quantity and proportion of that energy on maintaining social relations.

The question remains, though: in the relationship between energy and social complexity, which is cause and which is effect? White's Law, as seen above, would have energy usage as being the determinant of social complexity. Rambo (1991a), in contrast, sees a society's ability to harness energy as being dependent on its social complexity. He cites Service as being in agreement, as Service viewed the formation of more complex social structures to be dependent on "the evolution of more specialized means of integration." Sajise's (1991) observation that societies utilize social organization to establish patterns of resource allocation for the advantageous use of energy and information likewise places social complexity as the driving force in the relationship with energy.

Rather than declaring one side or the other to be wrong, it seems reasonable to posit the presence of a feedback mechanism. That is, as energy captured increases, a society has more ability to develop more effective means of social integration (for example, communication and enforcement of sanctions), which permits greater social complexity, and more ability to develop more technology. Greater social complexity and greater technology in turn enable the society to harness more energy.

These abstract arguments over the relationship between energy and social complexity have practical implications for the Manobo. If we acknowledge that money is a sort of "canned energy," it is evident that the Manobo will need more money as they develop greater social complexity. The point is readily seen in examining the Philippine government. Officials must spend money on hospitality to visitors, on communication with other officials, and on transportation. The expenses can be tremendous. In the rural areas, the government provides radios to the *barangay*, municipal, and provincial officials. A greater expense is transportation. Village officials may rely on public transportation, but *barangay* officials use government-provided motorcycles to get to their meetings, while mayors—who must travel farther, with an entourage—have government pickup trucks. Governors, congressmen, and senators make frequent use of air travel. On top of this, each year sees new agencies created to deal with new, specialized tasks. The cost of supporting government alone appears to increase faster than social complexity—and this ignores similar developments taking place in the private sector.

Agrophysical environment: Carrying capacity, population density, and technology

Several researchers have considered the "carrying capacity" of the environment to be a major determinant of culture. Fried, for instance, wrote, "One of the most important variables in the development of complex political systems is population size and density; these factors rest, in turn, upon the carrying capacity of the environment" (Rambo 1991b). Fried's position is supported by the case of the Pacific Northwest Native Americans, mentioned earlier, who were able to support a stratified society, despite relying on hunting and gathering, because of the rich supply of wild food available (Rambo 1991b). The principle of carrying capacity finds fuller development in the school of "cultural ecology," in which social organization is held to be a consequence of environmental situation, and social change a consequence of environmental change (Panya 1991). Panya names Clifford Geertz and Lucien Hanks as proponents of this approach, pointing to the example of Hanks' research on Bang Chan, a rural community in Thailand in which Hanks attributed the development of new technology by the residents there to land shortages caused by population increases. The concept is also supported by evidence from the Philippines. De Raedt (1991) observed that villages among the Ifugao are comprised of no more than 100 houses, due to the narrowness of land that can support irrigated rice production. In contrast, villages in Kalinga, where uninhabited land suitable for irrigated rice was still available, may have populations of up to 5,000.

While some researchers have concentrated on the limitations that environment places on population, Esther Boserup (1965:11–14) has demonstrated that higher population density frequently results in the development of new technology that facilitates more intensive use of the land. As with energy, there appears to be a feedback relationship between population and carrying capacity: a given environment can supply a limited quantity of resources to a society at a given time, due to its level of technology, which may limit population growth, but as population grows, higher population density lead the society to develop new technology that allows it to extract a greater quantity of resources from its environment.

Social forces

Discussion so far has focused on physical factors. However, social forces are also important, and become more important as societies become more complex (Rambo 1991b). For example, Panya's (1991) study of Thai farming practices between 1850 and 1950 revealed that changes in land use during this period, which had been attributed to limitations of the ecosystem, were actually due to pressure from Western countries to open Thailand to trade. The importance of social forces within societies is also significant. Marx and those who have followed him have brought out that differences in wealth—the existence of economic classes—give rise to differences in power. In contrast, Service (1993) has brought out that differences in power give rise to differences in economic position. "There really *was* inequality, always. Bands and tribes had unequal persons (but not segments). Chiefdoms and archaic civilizations were profoundly unequal, with regard to both individuals and segments. But the inequality was generated by the theocratic political system, which governed and controlled the economic system....[P]olitical institutions originated the economic system and controlled it." As with the issues of energy, carrying capacity, and technology, it seems most reasonable to accept that differences in economic position result in differences in power, and vice versa.

Cultural materialism

One prominent variant of cultural evolution theory is Marvin Harris' (1997:100–102) cultural materialism, which emphasizes constraints on culture due to material factors over those due to ideational factors. Harris divides culture into the three categories of infrastructure, structure, and superstructure. By infrastructure, he means the technologies and productive and reproductive activities that directly affect the satisfaction of material needs, as well as the society's agrophysical environment. Structure refers to the groups in society that control goods, labor, and information—that is, social structure. Superstructure refers to the society's mental culture (for example, beliefs, values, dances, songs, and religion). Harris holds that while each of these three elements of culture—infrastructure, structure, and superstructure—affects the emergence and retention or rejection of cultural innovations, infrastructure has the greatest effect of the three.

Paths of cultural evolution

While early theories of cultural evolution tended to posit single causes, later theories posited multilineal evolution. Service (Yengoyan 1991) attributed cultural evolution to several causes. "The actual evolution of the culture of particular societies is an adaptive process whereby the society solves problems with respect to the natural and to the human-competitive environment. These environments are so diverse, the problems so numerous, and the solutions potentially so various that no single determinant can be equally powerful for all cases" (Service 1968). Julian Steward likewise arrived at a multilineal approach (Rambo 1991b). Eder's (1991) research on the Negrito peoples of the Philippines suggests that they are not on a single continuum from forager to settled farmer, but rather that they have traveled a variety of different paths to arrive at their current situations. The complexity of societies' situations guarantees there will be no single, preordained path of cultural evolution. We can expect to find no single factor that is the sole force constraining or driving Manobo social organization. Instead, cultural evolution helps to suggest what forces will need to be considered, including energy, agrophysical environment, population, technology, and pressure from other groups and societies.

Emergence of horizontal and vertical integration

The presence of danger appears to engender the emergence of horizontal or vertical integration within societies. Lansing and de Vet (1999), for instance, compared the social organization of societies in the southern and northern portions of Nias, an Indonesian island off the southern coast of Sumatra, prior to 1900. Higher population levels in the south led to competition for land, resulting in inter-village war. In some portions of the area, residential units called *öri* arose that were governed by chiefs or nobles and bound together by means of mandatory feasts. The consequent horizontal and vertical integration provided mechanisms for defense and for maintaining agricultural productivity, giving the *öri* a competitive advantage over societies to the north. More convincing evidence comes from studies by Rambo (1991b) comparing societies of northern and southern Vietnam. The situation in the north was notably more dangerous than in the south, due to greater competition for resources, more frequent armed conflict, and more severe government coercion. Households in the north tended to join together in corporate groups, while those in the south were often independent of one another. Rambo reasoned that membership in a corporate group brought greater security, but only at a cost in both finances and reduction of freedom, and that those households at greater risk, as in the north, were willing to pay those costs.

Poggie (1995) came to similar conclusions when studying the relationship between cooperation in societies and food periodicity. He observed that cooperation was greatest in those societies that faced moderate urgency to harvest food. Cooperation enables people to accomplish tasks more quickly; thus, the less time available for harvest, the greater the need for cooperation. In cases where there was little urgency, there was little cooperation. However, extreme urgency also depressed cooperation, perhaps because the benefits of working with others came at too great an "opportunity cost" of not addressing one's own interests first. In a similar vein, Singelis et al. (1995) observed that in societies with status differentiation, the richest and poorest portions of the population tend to be individualistic, while the middle and lower classes tend to be collectivist. Apparently freedom from want eliminates the need to cooperate with others, while extreme pressure to survive eliminates the capacity to depend on others.

Intergroup conflict and the concentration of power

Richard Adams (1977) considers the adjustment of societies to power relationships with other societies to be the primary driving force behind cultural evolution. He has studied how groups utilize power to subordinate large segments of a society and how smaller societies respond to attempts at incorporation by larger ones. Adams' theory is based on the idea that each level of social complexity (band, chiefdom, state, or nation) is intrinsically tied to a particular level of control (that is, ability to make decisions). Independently of interaction with other societies, a society may increase in internal organization and move to a higher level of complexity through "pristine evolution." When confronted by another society, the society may develop a higher level of complexity in order to successfully fight back ("surgent evolution"). Alternatively, it may "integrate" into the more powerful and organized society, either retaining its original organization or becoming more organized. Or, it may be incorporated into the more powerful society and "disintegrate" (become less organized), in the process losing control over its own affairs and resources. Adams' paradigm reduces the number of possible interactions between two societies from an infinite variety to ten basic types, thereby making it easier to trace what is happening in a given situation and compare it to similar cases elsewhere.

Conflicts over land and natural resources

The national level

We now turn from social organization to consider one of the Manobo's most pressing problems: maintaining access to the land and natural resources on which they depend for survival. We will begin by considering policies and practices at the national level, as these determine how much latitude local populations have in managing natural resources.

As is true in most places, Philippine officials tend to be concerned about the financial health of their government and nation. However, as we have seen above, not all economic exchanges are monetized. In the subsistence situations common in remote areas, much of the economy is on a non-cash basis. Officials can readily dismiss these economies—and those who depend upon them—as unimportant. However, these subsistence economies are based on forests and marine areas of great value to the nation's livelihood. One wonders if the government might be motivated by desire to protect the wooded goose that is laying so many golden eggs.

Deforestation is a significant problem worldwide. Every year, the earth suffers a net loss of some 7.3 million hectares of forest (Forestry Department 2005:201), an area equal to half that of the state of Florida (Florida Netlink n.d.). The Philippines lost two-thirds of its forests between 1934 and 1998 (Oliva 1998), and is still losing around 157 km^2 per year (Forestry Department 2005:197). Unfortunately, those who pay the costs of forest loss often are not those who benefit. Indigenous populations in particular are often overlooked in the efforts of powerful, aggressive logging companies to make a profit (Human Rights Watch 1996; Lozano 1996).

This situation has its root in the Regalian Doctrine[4] by which the Philippine government claims rights to the Manobo's ancestral territory. The comments of Edmunds et al. (2003) are a pointed reply:

> [M]ost take for granted both the "public goods" interest of the state in forests and the legitimacy of government-sponsored devolution arrangements. We…instead…treat rights of local disadvantaged groups as primary, arguing for policy reforms that protect these local rights, while making incremental gains in protecting the public interest, rather than the reverse…Even where the rhetoric of poverty alleviation exists, such objectives have been framed in terms of meeting national objectives related to economic development, not in terms of protecting an individual's or community's right to economic self-determination. People living in forest areas, in particular, have been expected to cope with sometimes drastic limitations on their choices and to yield rights of self-determination commonly enjoyed by others living outside of forests.

Many officials have claimed that traditional farming techniques degrade the environment. Sanchez (1976:379), however, has reviewed numerous studies to show that traditional techniques are sustainable, and that

---

[4] The Philippine islands were under Spanish control from 1571 to 1896, when the colony revolted against Spain. The struggle for independence ended two years later when Spain ceded control of the islands to the United States at the close of the Spanish-American War. But while Spain lost control over the Philippines, its Regalian Doctrine—which holds that all land belongs to the government unless explicitly granted to private individuals—has remained part of Philippine law to the present time.

it is only when increased population density[5] forces swidden farmers to shorten the fallow period or when newcomers to an area attempt to utilize nonindigenous forms of agriculture that environmental degradation occurs. Sajise (1991) likewise notes that primitive subsistence systems have a high impact on the environment at the local level but a low impact at the watershed level, due to low population pressure. He further notes that while a shift from a subsistence to a cash economy usually results in forest degradation and agroecosystem instability, this has not been the case among several groups that have been able to exclude outsiders and therefore regulate the use of their own resources.

The Manobo's ability to govern their own territory may be aided by the passage in 1997 of Republic Act 8371, the Indigenous People's Rights Act (IPRA), which grants extensive rights over their ancestral lands to Philippine "indigenous cultural communities." The Philippine Supreme Court upheld IPRA after a protracted legal battle, but there continues to be significant opposition to the act, a situation Contreras (2003) expects to continue.

Resource management at the local level: Public, private, open-access, and common-pool arrangements

Having considered the national context, we now turn to a consideration of how resources may be managed. Many have taken their cue from Garrett Hardin's (1968) story of the "tragedy of the commons," in which each cattle owner, concerned about his own interests only, stocks as many head as possible on the village commons, in the process reducing overall production from the land. Many concluded from Hardin's illustration that the only alternative to unregulated use of "common property" is private ownership. Unfortunately, this analysis seriously errs in overlooking other viable alternatives (Ostrom 1990:1–21). Hunt and Gilman (1998) define four approaches to resource management:
- open access, in which access is open to all
- common property, in which access is open only to group members
- private property, in which access is controlled by the owner
- public property, in which access is controlled by the state

Ostrom (1990:222) warns that many people fail to distinguish between the first two arrangements, and restricts the term "common property resource" (CPR) to the second arrangement.

Berkes (1989a) suggests that neither overexploitation nor sustained use is inevitable, but that it depends upon the social situation. He observed that sustainable use is much more likely among peoples living in small, tightly knit groups that have firm communal control over the resource and over

---

[5] In the case of the Manobo, increased population density was due to the arrival of settlers.

social behavior. He is essentially saying that a CPR arrangement is likely to work in a high-group society. Ostrom (1990:41–43) states that in the case of firms or states, an entrepreneur or ruler takes on the burden of arranging collective action, who keeps a substantial portion of the surplus thereby generated for himself. He therefore has an interest in making credible threats against anyone breaking the cooperative arrangement or damaging his property. As some of the surplus is left to the others in the group, they find their net position an improvement over independent existence and therefore continue with the arrangement. Thus, in the case of private or public property, sustainability is maintained through vertical integration.

Berkes (1989a) observes that "tragedies of the commons" seem to be the exception rather than the rule, and usually occur when an outside power disrupts existing CPR systems. Large areas of forest had been success-fully managed by Indian communities in pre-colonial times, but after the arrival of the British, many village commons were transformed into pri-vate property, while extensive areas of forest were commercially logged (Berkes 1989b). In areas where the state has not intervened, there have been numerous cases of successful common property resource management (Ostrom 1990:64–67). She suggests two conditions as necessary for success-ful CPR arrangements: populations that remain stable over long periods of time, and situations that are uncertain and complex (Ostrom 1990:88–91). With stable populations, individuals can expect to benefit from charita-ble behavior toward others, and can expect any investments to pay off to themselves or their heirs. Ostrom's suggestion that uncertain and complex situations favor CPR arrangements is consistent with my earlier conclusion (pp. 14–15) that moderate danger facilitates the emergence of horizontal and vertical integration. She has identified eight specific characteristics that appear to be common to enduring CPR arrangements:

- clearly defined boundaries, of both the membership and the resource itself
- reasonable rules
- participation in decisions open to most members
- monitoring
- progressively severe sanctions
- conflict-resolution mechanisms
- governmental recognition of right to govern the resource
- a nested organizational structure, in the case of large systems.

Cultural specifics: Cues to the Manobo's use of social structures for supradomestic cooperation

We now turn from theories of social organization and resource management to specifics of culture. There are several excellent treatments of the social organization and related features of the less socially complex societies of insular Southeast Asia and of mainstream Philippine society. Examples are

Jocano (1969, 1997, 1998a, 1998b), Lingenfelter (1990), Kerr (1988a), Allison (1984), Mayers (1980), Hollnsteiner, ed. (1979), Schlegel (1970, 1979), Drucker (1974), Manuel (1973), Hudson (1972), Frake (1960), and Garvan (1941). As interesting as these are, I will refrain from giving a detailed description of these societies and will instead highlight a few points that are especially significant to an understanding of the Manobo's use of social structures for supradomestic cooperation. (See "Significant Publications on the Cotabato Manobo" in appendix C for additional resources on the Cotabato Manobo and the other Manobo peoples of Mindanao.)

Philippine societies are characterized by patron-client relationships (Arce 1979; Lynch 1979a), negotiated social relationships (Hollnsteiner 1979a), the avoidance of face-to-face confrontation (Arce and Poblador 1979), and the basing of relationships on person rather than office (Szanton 1979). These observations were made with regard to "lowland" Philippine society, but are in large measure applicable to Philippine peoples generally. In many of the socially less-complex societies of Borneo, there are no stable groups other than the household, which is frequently limited to the nuclear family. In these societies, kinship serves as the starting point for recruitment to ephemeral groups, an observation that Hollnsteiner (1979b), Arce (1979), and Lynch (1979b) make for Philippine societies. An arrangement in the Philippines of particular note is that of the *sukì* relationship. Szanton's (1979) description of the relationship as seen among Ilonggos (a Philippine people) appears typical of practice in several other locations. The word is used of both parties in a market relationship (that is, vendor and customer) and is probably best translated as "regular exchange partner." The relationship is often long lasting and is based on personal reciprocity. Szanton's observation that the *sukì* relationship is pervasive in Philippine economic life suggests it may be mirrored in Philippine politics—that is, the receipt of some service or favor from an official is equivalent to buying from a particular vendor. The official tends to expect continued "loyalty," while the constituent tends to expect special attention. Government offices tend to be run under a "patronage" system.

Summary

Like many indigenous peoples around the world, the Manobo have in recent decades been strongly impacted by powerful outside forces. These forces have produced profound changes in their culture, including the way they organize their social, political, and economic relations. Yet the Manobo are not the mere object of these forces, plastically conforming to the pressures placed upon them, for the organizational patterns they have developed in response to pressure from the outside enable them to exert pressure on the very parties affecting them. I have drawn from theories of cultural evolution and power configurations within and between societies in order to investigate the effect of external forces upon the Manobo and the Manobo's response to these forces. Cultural evolution focuses on causal interactions, emphasizing either the political or the economic. Some theorists have focused on the impact of the behavior of the state, anticipating that external power intrusions will lead to internal power rearrangements; others have focused on the effect of changes in technology and the economic base, holding that they will lead to changes in social organization and the idea system.

Several theories focus on configurations of social interaction and the relationship of these to power: social network analysis, social capital, grid-group theory, and Richard Adams' theory of competition between societies. (Theories regarding common-pool resources may be regarded as an applied variant, in that they relate property regime to social configuration.) Taken together, these theories add depth to that of cultural evolution by their focus on the mechanisms by which political and material pressures produce specific social organization configurations and associated idea systems. Perhaps even more importantly, they bring out that social organization and idea systems are not merely the products of state influence and the material environment but are also the means by which societies act on the state and their biophysical environment.

The combination of these two schools of thought thus allows for feedback relationships between the state, the biophysical/economic environment, and the Manobo's social organization and idea system. Given the similarity between the Manobo's situation and that of many other indigenous peoples, it is anticipated that the principles elucidated from this combined approach to the analysis of the Manobo's situation will be theoretically pertinent to land and natural resource conflicts in many other locations.

2

Before the Woodsman's Coming: Life in Isolation Pre-1953

The physical setting

Before examining how the Manobo have adapted to the new situation that has been thrust upon them, we need to begin with a "baseline." What was life like before the changes came flooding in? We will begin with a description of the Manobo's physical world, which provided the resources they relied on; then examine their traditional economic system; and conclude with a look at the role of internal migration in their traditional system.

The Cotabato Manobo are a small indigenous minority within the Philippines. They number around 30,000 (Lewis et al. 2015a), compared to a national population of about 100 million (Population Reference Bureau 2015). Traditionally, they subsisted on root crops, rice, and maize, which they produced using shifting cultivation. The Manobo live in the highlands of the large southern island of Mindanao. Their territory once extended from the coast into the inland mountains, but most of the Manobo have been displaced from the coastal areas. Their current habitat is therefore largely one of steep mountains cut by rivers and streams. The vegetation is high forest covering a thin, dark topsoil. The soil is moderately productive until the subsoil—a heavy, sticky orange clay—is exposed, at which point agricultural yields drop sharply.

Rainfall is around 2,100 mm per year.[1] The area experiences a pronounced dry season from January through March. Rains begin in April,
are heaviest in June and July, and taper off in August and September. Some
rain continues to fall in October through December, though not as much.

Biological aspects of the Manobo economy

Swidden agriculture

Accounts[2] from older members of Manobo society indicate that their territory was once almost entirely forested. Before settlers (as defined in the
preface) began arriving from other parts of the Philippines, triggering the
changes we will examine in this book, the Manobo supported themselves
through swidden agriculture,[3] supplemented by hunting and gathering.
Sulutan Edod Nayam,[4] a resident of Elem, illustrated life as it used to be
with an account of one of his ancestors, Datù Muluk. The account will be
familiar to those acquainted with the major phases of the swidden cycle.

> [He had eight dogs.] He went spear-hunting for deer and pig
> and caught four deer. When he saw the land he decided to cut a
> swidden there. He and his followers planted many things. When
> they harvested the maize, they stored it on a loosely woven bamboo
> fence (*kinentoy*) [figure 2.1]. He planted two seasons, then told his
> followers they should plant in a new area, as there were now too
> many weeds for the women to handle.
>   Various useful wild plants grew up in the abandoned field,
> including rattan heart and palm heart, which could be harvested
> when they became mature.

---

[1] Rainfall in the Philippines varies substantially from one area to another, and data
have been collected for only a few localities. The national average rainfall of 2451
mm (Youngblood-Coleman, n.d.) is probably similar to that of the Manobo area.

[2] My reconstruction of the Manobo's traditional way of life is based on interviews
with 51 informants (12 women and 39 men), mostly taken between June 2005 and
October 2006 and between September 1994 and May 1995.

[3] Anthropologists may be more accustomed to saying the Manobo practiced
"horticultural." However, to Americans working in crop production, and probably to
the American populace at large, "agriculture" denotes farming, while "horticulture"
denotes the production of expensive specialty crops such as flowers, other
ornamentals, and fruits. At the same time, use of the term "swidden farming" is
problematic, as farming implies the existence of farms, which in American usage
are understood to have a fixed location. I will use the term "swidden agriculture" as
what seems to be the best compromise. I will also use the term "agriculture" to refer
to crop production.

[4] The Manobo words *datù* and *sulutan* refer to traditional leaders, with *sulutan*
considered the more prestigious title. I have italicized the terms when they are used as
words, but left them in regular type when they are used as titles with a proper noun.

The old people told them what trees not to remove: *tepek, kedies, tubang, belengahal, belangas,* and *saging ubal.* Instead, they were to cut down trees that had no use, like *tungow.* Don't cut down trees that produce fruit.

Now, about rattan. [He named several kinds, including *limulan.*] Why did we know those? Because we depended on them. We learned the names from our parents.

People's areas were previously separated by mountains, ridges, and waterways. These provided natural boundaries between areas. We didn't have "released land" or *sinintù iglebeng* [concrete markers buried in the ground], just mountains and ridges and waterways.

Figure 2.1. A *kinentoy*, an arrangement in which maize ears are hung on a loosely woven bamboo fence.

The Manobo have continued to practice swidden agriculture, when they are allowed to, though the central element in that land use system, the felling of trees for land clearing purposes, has been greatly curtailed by the logging company active in their area. Such restrictions, of course, bring no ecological benefits to the region, as the purpose of the restrictions is not to protect the forest, but to protect the company's right to cut trees. The removal of trees by logging is far more drastic than that in the Manobo's traditional swidden system. In terms of economic impact on Manobo lifeways, the catastrophic impact of the restrictions against tree cutting will be discussed later. The present paragraphs simply describe the processes involved in the traditional system.

Preparation of the swidden is considered men's work.[5] Each man cuts an area of forest in January, when the dry season begins. The Manobo now

[5] The Manobo distinguish between two kinds of swiddens. This section refers to the *tinibah* (meaning "an area that has been cleared"), the type of swidden upon which the Manobo have relied for most of their food. The *tinibah* is planted in March to a mixture of crops. The Manobo also sometimes plant a *pelusak*, a type of swidden

use axes or *kelu* (large, recurved field knives), but the oldest men remember using the *kulut*, a lightweight predecessor to the axe (figures 2.2a–e). Very little rain falls during January and February, allowing the vegetation to dry. The cleared area is burned in February and then planted in February and March, once the rains begin. Much of the area is planted to maize[6] and rice.

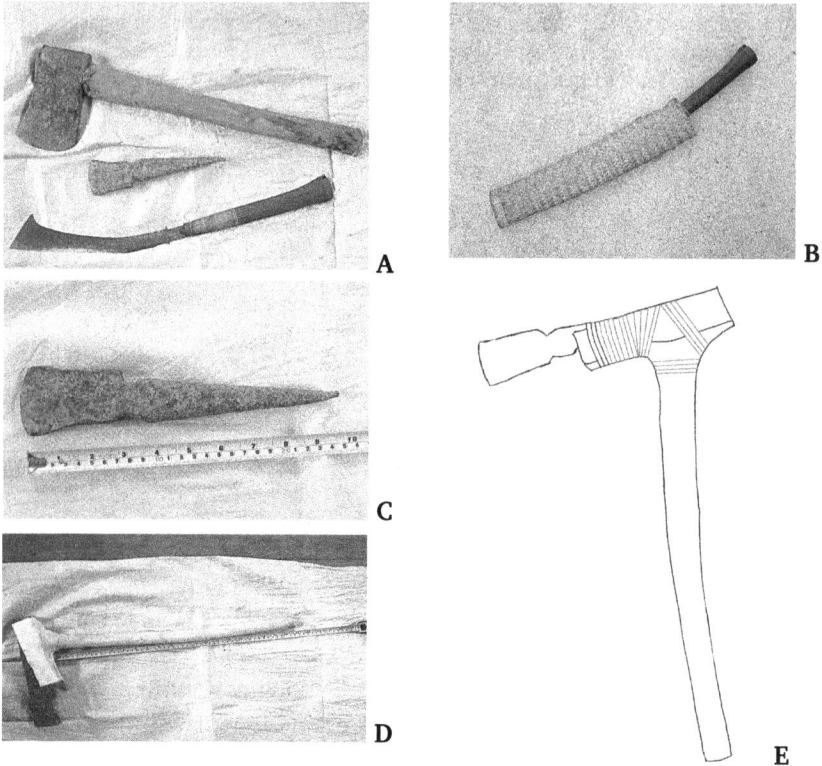

Figure 2.2. Traditional farming implements.
A) *Agsà*, *kulut*, and *kelu*. B) *Kelu* (field knife) in *gumà* (sheath). The sheath is woven from rattan. C) *Kulut* blade. D) *Kulut* blade and handle.
E) *Kulut*, with blade bound to handle.

---

they consider to be a supplement to the *tinibah*. The *pelusak* is distinguished from the *tinibah* by being planted about the same time as rice harvest (near the end of August) and being planted solely to maize.

[6] Maize, as is common knowledge, originated in Latin America (Martin et al. 1976:325). It was presumably brought to the Philippines during the Spanish era, as was cassava (Martin et al. 1976:947), and their high yield and adaptability to the climate led to their dissemination throughout the archipelago. Grain sorghum and pearl millet are thought to have originated in Africa (Martin et al. 1976:386, 570), while foxtail millet was grown in China as early as 2700 BC (Martin et al. 1976:563). These crops may have been brought to the Philippines with Chinese merchants, or by Arab traders

Tradition was followed carefully when planting. Merlinda, a female informant, explained that planting of the maize began each year with the seed from a single ear. Once this is planted, the people went home, and then returned the next day to plant the remainder of the area. The women plant the maize in a random pattern using a dibble stick, with some 1.5 meters (two paces) between hills. A few days later, when the maize has sprouted and can be seen, men interplant the area with rice seed. Like the maize, the rice is planted in a random pattern using a dibble stick. An aged male informant, Kalah of Elem, added that he used to clear three separate fields, and that when he planted, he first planted a small portion for Nemula, the Creator, in order to honor Him, because the land belongs to Him. Only then did he plant his own.

Among the women I interviewed, ranging in age from a mother in her late 20s to grandmothers in their late 40s, their husbands (or in one divorcée's case, her brother) cleared the land they planted. The women planted. In polygynous households, the co-wives help each other plant. The wives might give each other seed. Or, one wife might borrow seed from her co-wife and repay the same amount when she harvests.

Traditional varieties were used for both the maize and rice. The traditional maize varieties, called *tigtu kelang* (real maize), are glutinous and mildly sweet with multicolored ears, and require only two and one-half to three months from planting till harvest, depending on the variety. There were two general types of traditional rice varieties. *Dakel palay* (large rice) can grow as tall as one's shoulder and takes five to seven months from planting until harvest in September. *Belowon* takes only four months from planting until harvest.

In addition to maize and rice, other crops were planted in the swidden as well, including cassava, tropical yam, taro, yautia, grain sorghum, and millet.[7] Grain sorghum was sometimes planted around houses to repel *tuyang busaw* (a demon's dog).[8] The *tuyang busaw* was believed to avoid the grain sorghum, as the crop's seedhead resembles the dog's tail. Millet is boiled into a porridge. The grain can also be burned and the ash rubbed on skin affected by stinging caterpillars or other irritating hairs. Vegetables and condiments were also planted, including eggplant, cowpeas, squash, basil, and lemongrass.

---

by way of India and the Malaysian archipelago. Maize, cassava, sorghum, and millet are thus all "exotic" crops. However, even my oldest informants cannot recall a time that these crops were not used by their people, or even stories of such a time. The crops are thus appropriately considered part of the Manobo's traditional cropping system.

[7] The word "millet" refers to any of a number of small-seeded annual cereal crops. The Manobo word *betem*, which I have glossed "millet," may be foxtail millet or pearl millet.

[8] *Tuyang busaw* means "demon's dog." Like demons (*busaw*), it is usually invisible and immaterial, but can interact with the physical world and can sometimes be seen.

Traditionally, the ears of maize were cut from the stalk in such a way that a short length of stalk remained attached to the base of the ear, forming a hook. Using this, the ears—still in the husk—were hung out in the open on a woven bamboo fence, the bottom of which was a few feet off the ground (figure 2.1). This arrangement, which the Manobo call a *kinentoy*, allowed the grain to dry while minimizing damage from moisture and insects. The maize husks shed rain from the ears like a thatched roof and kept weevils from spreading from one ear to another. At the same time, the ears' exposure to sunlight helped them dry. While the *kinentoy* system probably takes more labor than the Latin American practice, it may also provide better rat control, as rodents are reticent to expose themselves to hawks and owls by climbing on the exposed ears. The grain was shelled from the ear by hand as needed and ground into grits using a mortar and pestle.

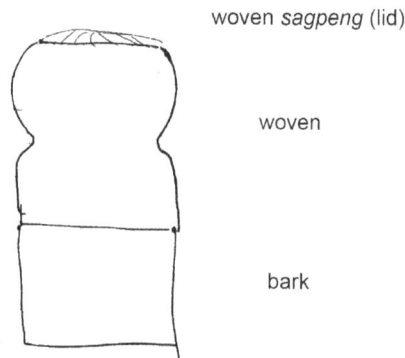

woven *sagpeng* (lid)

woven

bark

Figure 2.3. A *lihub*, used for storing rice.

The mature rice was pulled from the stalk by hand.[9] After drying in the sun, the grain (with husk attached) was placed in large containers called *lihub* (figure 2.3) made of bark that had been stripped from the *kalah* tree. The bark was sewn together using rattan, and a rattan "net" was constructed as the bottom of the container. Rice straw was then placed in the

---

[9] The Manobo quite literally pulled rice from the stalk by hand prior to the 1930s and 1940s. They later adopted use of the *langgaman*, a blade pressed against the palm (p. 62), to strip the rice head from the stalk, but harvested without tools before that. Conklin (1975:113) observed the same behavior among the Hanunóo people of Mindoro, an island in the central Philippines. He reported, "Optionally, [as an alternative to harvesting by hand]...metal blades for transverse rice harvesting knives (*yatab*) may be forged or repaired and set in new wooden handles. This usage is not obligatory, however, and in most cases all rice harvesting is by hand. The *yatab* has been known to the Hanunóo for several generations, but it is still considered a foreign, Christian implement, and for this reason, somewhat less suited than the bare hands" (Conklin 1975:113).

bottom and along the sides and the dried rice grain placed inside. When the container was full, the Manobo placed a layer of rice straw on top and tied it in with another rattan "net." A family might have one or several of these *lihub*. Seed for the next year would be set aside in a smaller container and was not considered available to eat. The Manobo would occasionally open the *lihub* to determine whether the grain was spoiling from excess moisture and, if necessary, dry it and then return it to the *lihub*. Rice was prepared for eating by pounding in a mortar and pestle to loosen the husk from the grain, winnowed to remove the husk, and then boiled.

The traditional cropping system was designed to extend the harvest season, thereby supplying food over more of the year. While most of the maize and rice was harvested as mature grain, a portion was eaten while still "green." Maize was eaten as boiling ears in June, and then as roasting ears, after which it becomes too dry and hard to eat fresh. Likewise, a small portion of the rice is harvested once it has matured but is too moist to store. The green rice is parched (roasted without oil in a frying pan) and then pounded, winnowed, and boiled as usual. The cropping season was also extended by using two varieties of maize. *Dakel kelang* (large maize) is still in the boiling ear stage in June, while *mepokò belus* (short-silked [maize]) is already too mature to eat even as roasting ears.

The Manobo have traditionally reckoned planting time by the stars using *Dakel Bituen* (the "Big Star," Canis Major), *Telu* (the "Three," Orion's Belt), and *Putel* (the Pleiades). An additional guideline that one informant followed is to plant at the full moon so that his rice, like the moon, would be full. The informants say their ancestors used to cut their fields in January, burn in February, and plant in March.[10]

While planting time was dictated by the stars, a field's location was guided by omens. Of particular importance was the *limuken,* the white-eared brown dove. The dove tells one if it is safe to prepare a field in a particular place. The farmer clears a small area within the proposed swidden, and then places his backpack[11] on the ground and calls out to the dove and asks it to tell him if it will be safe to make a field there. If the dove responds, then the man knows it is all right to go ahead. However, if the dove's call comes from in front, it is a warning that if the farmer goes ahead and makes a field there, someone will die, and the people will not get to eat the crop. If that omen happens, people would not farm there, even if the dove had previously given a favorable omen. The informants said that is why their ancestors used to make fields in so many places: if they started to

---

[10] The Western Bukidnon Manobo reckoned planting time using a similar method (Hires and Headland 1977).

[11] I am referring not to a purchased backpack such as college students or recreational campers use, but to the *puyut,* a small backpack in which men typically carry small personal items, such as the makings for betel nut chew.

prepare a field in one place and received an unfavorable omen, they would start over in another place.

After the rice was harvested, a swidden was sometimes replanted to supplement the food supply. In this practice, known as *kandulì*, the men cleared the field of weeds, after which the women planted a variety of crops (maize, yams, cassava, yautia, sugar cane, and taro) using a dibble stick. This second planting occurred in September.

The crops were subject to numerous pests. Some pests (fire ants; the *bekuku*, a dove similar to the *limuken*; and the chestnut munia birds) eat rice seed out of the field. A variety of rodents eat the immature panicle inside the rice stalk, while munias eat the grain once it begins to mature. Maize is subject to attack by rats, doves, wild pigs, and monkeys. The wild pigs also eat root and tuber crops. There were also insect pests, including the rice stink bug, mole cricket, and cutworm. The Manobo had ways of dealing with many of these problems. Pigs could often be excluded by fences built from bamboo and rattan. Birds were scared away using scarecrows and bamboo noisemakers, operated by rattan lines (figure 2.4). Monkeys were especially clever pests and had to be driven off by shouting at them. Occasionally a man could get close enough to kill one with bow and arrow.

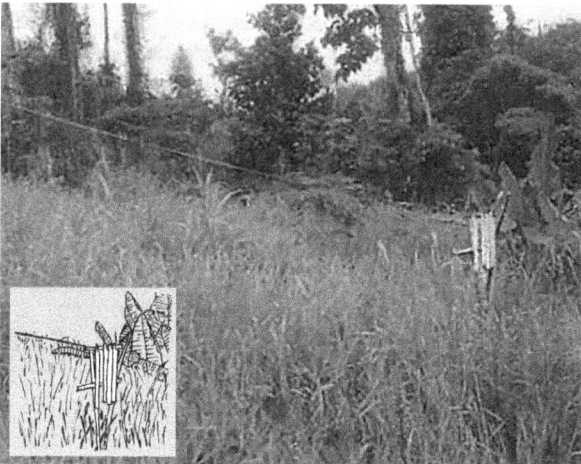

Figure 2.4. Noisemaker, to scare away birds.
Photograph and close-up drawing (inset).

While animal pests were troublesome, the greatest difficulty seems to have been weeds. These included buffalo grass, goosegrass, beggar's tick, and pigweed. The deep shade under the forest canopy effectively controlled weeds until the field was cleared, and burning of the dried plant material killed any remaining weed species, and provided nutrients[12] to the soil as

---

[12] The ash produced from the burned plant materials contains a number of inorganic elements, including phosphorus, potassium, calcium, and a number of micronutrients.

well. After the crops emerged the fields were weeded by hand. After one or two seasons, however, the weeds became increasingly numerous, and the Manobo abandoned their fields and moved on to open new areas of forest.[13]

The Manobo have varied in how long they allow the forest to regenerate before using an area again for farming. Informants gave figures ranging from seven to over fifty years. The Manobo have used—and continue to use—indicator species to find fertile regrowth areas. Among these are lantana and *budakan*, a vine in the mallow family having large, heart-shaped leaves.

Once an area of forest is cleared and planted, it immediately begins to return to climax forest. Harold Conklin (1975) has documented that the Hanunóo people of Mindoro, in the central Philippine islands, deliberately mimicked the natural succession back to climax forest through the crops they planted. The Hanunóo planted newly cleared swiddens to a mixture of annual crops, along with more slowly maturing crops such as cassava, yams, sweet potatoes, yautia, and taro. The more slowly maturing crops were either bushy (cassava) or climbing crops (yams and sweet potato), or able to tolerate shade (yautia and taro)—precisely the kind of plants that take over an abandoned field. The Hanunóo also planted their fields with papaya, bananas, and various fruit trees. These grow more slowly than the cassava and yams, but begin to pass them in height as the cassava and yams mature. Tall forest species are allowed to grow up among the fruit trees, eventually shading out the fruit trees, but not before they provide several years of food. The Manobo's system appears to have some of the same characteristics. The Manobo plant a similar mixture of slow-growing taller crops with annual crops. Papaya is allowed to volunteer in cleared fields, along with *selawì* (a vining legume with a seed like that of lima beans). The Manobo also plant fruit trees in their fields, including jackfruit, which provides lumber as well as fruit.

Gathering

The forest has also been important to the Manobo as a source of wild greens and staples, fibers, building materials, and medicinal herbs. Even now, the women gather a number of wild greens, including wild fern, *utan* (a vine with a bitter leaf), and beggar's tick. Rattan heart and bamboo sprouts provide variety to the diet, while wild betel nut has played the same gustatory and social

---

[13] My informants said that, while soil fertility did decrease over time, they moved to new areas because of weed pressure. This is consistent with the findings of Pedro Sanchez (1976:378), who after extensive study of tropical agricultural systems was of the opinion that "The need for weed control may be the primary reason why fields are abandoned in high-base-status soils, whereas fertility depletion may be the primary cause in lower-base-status soils." The limestone-derived clay loam soils of the Manobo area likely have relatively high base status in the A horizon, which would be not be substantially eroded under shifting cultivation.

role that coffee and tea do in many other cultures. The forest has also provided staples before the rice matured, or when crops had failed because of drought or other cause. The Manobo have harvested a variety of wild root and tuber crops, including *biking* (a wild yam) and *kelut* (another wild yam, poisonous if not processed by long leaching in running water). The Manobo also extracted starch from a large palm called *basag*. The tree was felled and split open and the pith dug out with adzes fashioned on the spot from bamboo (figure 2.5a–c). The shredded pith was mixed with water and poured down a banana-stalk trough, where the starch settled out. The starch was then heated over a fire until it congealed and wrapped with banana leaf wrappers to be eaten later.

A & B

C

Figure 2.5. Extracting starch from palm pith.
A) Shredding palm pith B) Close-up of shredding palm pith.
Next, shredded palm pith is treaded to extract starch, settled starch is
scooped from the bark trough, and the starch is roasted.
C) Dividing up the starch after roasting.

While wild foods helped to supplement the food from crops, drought occasionally made life very difficult. The Manobo tell of people sucking water from rotten wood during a drought before World War II. Most of the springs dried up, but one continued to flow at a place that came to be called *Linesedan*, meaning "the fenced-off place." Anyone who came to drink there had to leave something in payment. Many left spears (at that time essential for hunting, and heirlooms), stabbing them in the ground near the water. Over time, the water was surrounded with a "fence" of spears, giving the place its name.

The Manobo made use of a number of non-timber forest products (NTFPs), and—when the plants are available—continue to do so. The forest contains a number of species of bamboo. *Apus*, a very large, thick-walled bamboo, provides material for flooring. *Kawayan* and *bolò*, thin-walled species, provide material to make woven walling. *Belèkayu*, a small bamboo with a narrow lumen, is used for arrow shafts. There are also climbing bamboos, chief of which is *napnap*, used for weaving baskets for tasks as varied as carrying crops from field to house, to fishing, to making a sheath or scabbard for field knives (cf. figure 2.2). Rattan was used instead of nails in building houses, and to construct thatched roofs from cogon grass, bamboo, and wooden poles.

Other plants provided rope and clothing. The Manobo strip fibers from the stalk of abaca and roll them between palm and thigh into cords. These are still used for the belt from which men suspend their field knife sheaths, and were previously sewn into blankets. Abaca cords were laid side by side and stitched together with abaca thread using a bamboo needle. Bark cloth, at one time used for breechcloths, was made from the bark of the *kalah* tree. Two cuts were made around the trunk and the bark stripped from the tree. The bark was soaked in water and pounded until only the phloem fibers remained, producing a thick fabric.

Wild plants have also provided the Manobo with a number of herbal remedies. The bark from one tree[14] has been used to treat malaria. The conical flower heads from *mekepenù*, a plant in the aster family, are chewed and applied to toothache; they provide a potent but short-lived anaesthetic effect. The flowers of *pungpung*, another plant in the aster family, are rubbed between the hands and their fragrance inhaled as an antidote to lightheadedness.

In summary, the Manobo's traditional means of obtaining plant sustenance relied on swidden agriculture, supplemented by gathering of wild plants and of "weeds" that grew in cultivated fields during their succession back to forest. However, this traditional system was to be subjected to tremendous pressure to change when the Philippine government opened their territory to settlers and logging companies.

Hunting, trapping, and fishing

While plant materials provided the Manobo with energy, their traditional crops could not supply everything they needed for adequate nutrition. As

---

[14] I have not seen this plant and do not know its botanical identity.

was the case in pre-colonial Mesoamerica, grain and root crops provided a dependable source of carbohydrates, but to obtain adequate protein they continued to rely on a more ancient system based on hunting, trapping, and fishing. As Sulutan Edod Nayam explained:

> If we don't have food, we get food from the forest: *biking* and *lodon* [a plant that has "fruit" in the ground] and rattan [heart]. We catch wild pigs with spear traps. We also trap monkeys [with pointed stakes]. We catch deer with spear traps. We catch pigs with deadfalls. This is what our ancestors taught us. When we caught something, we would call our companions together and divide the catch according to how many wives each man had. Each man took as many parcels as the number of wives he had. If someone else caught something, then they would call me to get my share.

Pigs and deer were also hunted using dogs and spears, with several men cooperating in the hunt. Dogs would track the quarry and keep it at bay while the men ran through the forest, following the dogs' howls. Once they came upon their quarry, they would kill it with spear thrusts, and then divide the meat among those taking part in the hunt. This sharing of produce was less common in the case of domesticated crops, where each family harvested and consumed its own food. But intracommunal sharing was the norm in that protein-procurement sector of the economy based on the hunting and trapping of wild animals, particularly mammalian species.[15]

The forest previously supported a wide variety of birds, including hornbills, coletos, small wood-peckers, slender-billed crows, Philippine eagles, white-eared brown doves, and blue-breasted quail. However, many are now seen less often than even ten years ago. There were also a number of species of wild mammals, including Philippine palm civets, monkeys, Philippine tarsiers, several rodents, wild pigs, deer, and various species of bats. As with the birds, these are less common now than before. The largest predators are pythons and crocodiles. However, pythons are rare, and crocodiles are limited to areas near large bodies of water, so not a concern in most parts of Manobo territory. There are also a large number of other reptiles, including several poisonous and non-poisonous snakes, and lizards.

The Manobo have traditionally hunted pig and deer with spears, using dogs to track and corner the quarry. Many of the men who have hunted have broken toes from barefoot pursuit over the steep and uneven terrain. The Manobo also catch pigs using pits lined with sharpened stakes, deadfalls, and spear traps. Small mammals and birds are trapped using snares. The Manobo make a particularly ingenious trap from bamboo, the *tekob* (figure 2.6a–f), to catch wild rodents. One of the species caught with it is the *mebulà*

---

[15] Interestingly, the !Kung of the Kalahari Desert observe a similar distinction between meat and plant products. While the !Kung share both gathered and hunted foods (Lee 1979:118), game meat is shared more widely in the community than plant products and small animals obtained by gathering (Marshall 1976:357–363).

ikug ("white tail"), a large rat with a white tail that makes trails through corn fields but does little damage to the crop. The Manobo do not eat house rats.

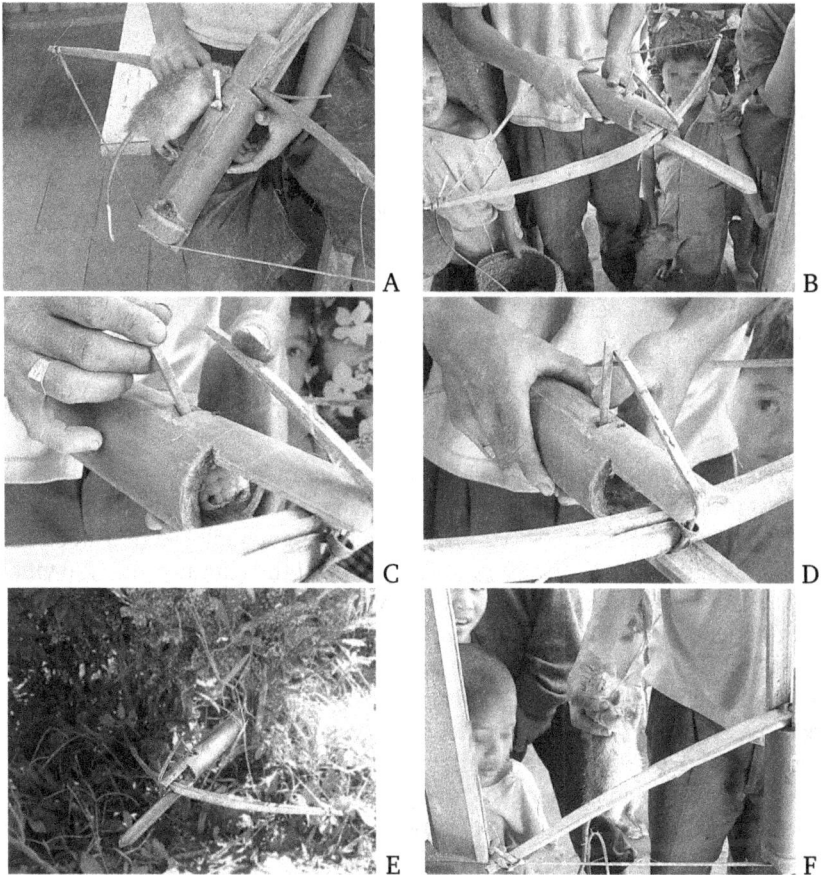

Figure 2.6. *Tekob* (bamboo rat traps).
A) The *tekob*, with captured *mebulà ikug*. B) Close-up of the *tekob*.
C) Baiting the trap. D) Trigger mechanism. E) Baited trap, set in the field.
F) The catch. Built and demonstrated by Amay Doyén.

The Manobo now catch fish and eels with purchased steel hooks, but also employ several methods developed before they had extensive commercial contact with mainstream Philippine society. It is common to catch fresh-water eels by hand, feeling carefully under rocks in the creek beds and grabbing the eel before it can escape. The Manobo sometimes make rock dams across mountain streams to dry up the watercourse and leave the fish stranded on the streambed; the fish are then collected by hand. Various plants are used to poison fish, which are collected when they float to the surface. The Manobo also make fish traps from bamboo. These are placed in waterways with the mouth pointing upstream. The fish swim into the mouth and down a funnel into the trap, but cannot swim out again because of the sharpened bamboo pieces at the bottom of the funnel.

Domestic animals

At one time, the only animal the Manobo raised for meat was the chicken. Many Manobo now raise domestic pigs, but they are a more recent addition. Ducks are uncommon and even more recent. On the other hand, the horse and carabao appear to have played a part in the Manobo economy for some time. Older men list both animals as part of the brideprice (*songgud*) they gave when married, and the horse was a frequent item of payment (*tamuk*) in *antang*, conflict settlements negotiated between *datù*. Carabao are now valued as draft animals as well, but in the past were used solely as part of the brideprice.

Technological aspects of the Manobo economy

Prior to the arrival of settlers, the Manobo economy functioned largely in isolation from mainstream Philippine society. What items came from the outside were often obtained through barter. The technology employed depended little on materials from the outside. Amay Tiya,[16] one of the oldest men in the village of Pokò Wayeg, estimates he was twelve years old when he saw the Japanese and American planes fighting during World War II; he was still unmarried. He relates that when he was young, the only metal tool they had was the *kulut*; no one as yet had field knives (*kelu*), drop hoes, or hammers. They used rattan to bind houses together instead of nails. However, they did have *sundang* (a short sword with wavy blade), obtained from the Maranao people to the north of Manobo territory and exchanged throughout the language group as brideprice.

Metalworking appears to have come to the Manobo about the same time that settlers began to arrive. Amay Tiya already had two wives when the first Manobo blacksmith in the region of Pokò Wayeg, Amay Empung, began making *kelu*. As Amay Tiya was unmarried at the outbreak of World War II, and perhaps as late as the close of the war, this places the beginning of metalwork in the Pokò Wayeg area as the late 1940s or early 1950s. Amay Puto, the second person in the area to smith, learned that skill directly from Amay Empung. Amay Puto is considered old, but is still able to smith.

Older informants recall making bark cloth from the *kalah* and *lakeg* and *beluwanà* trees. This was used for blankets and breechcloths, or sewn into shorts using bamboo needles. The women covered their breasts with *bangì*[17] leaves and their

---

[16] Adults with children are frequently referred to by their teknonym as a matter of respect. Amay Tiya means "father of Tiya." Tiya's mother would be called Inay Tiya.

[17] *Bangì* is a monocot with long, somewhat narrow leaves. If the Manobo word refers to the same plant as the identical word in the closely related Tasaday language, *bangì* is *Curculigo capitulata*, a member of the Amaryllidaceae (Yen and Gutierrez 1976:127).

genitalia with coconut shells. Sometime after World War II the Manobo began obtaining the now-ubiquitous *lobing* (*sari* or tube-skirt; Tagalog *malong*) through exchange for the resin of the white lauan tree, and through purchase after selling rice. The Manobo also began buying flour sacks and making clothing from them.

Metal cooking implements were not used before World War II, when the older informants were young. Rice was sometimes cooked by wrapping a small quantity in a *lekék*[18] leaf, placing the wrapped bundle in a section of bamboo with a small amount of water, and heating the bamboo by a low fire (figure 2.7a–f). The Manobo also cooked rice in earthen pots made from dark red clay. Cooking was accomplished by placing rice and water in the pots and then adding stones that had been heated in a fire.

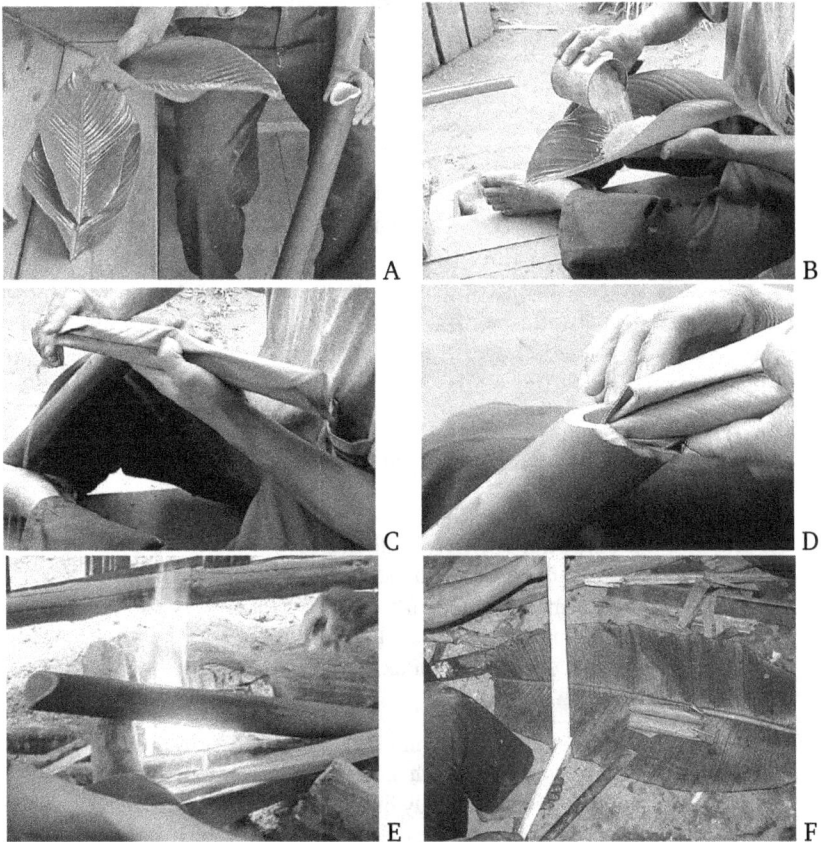

Figure 2.7. *Linulù* (rice cooked by steaming in bamboo).
A) Bamboo section and *lekék* leaves. B) Pouring raw rice into *lekék* leaf.
C) Wrapping *lekék* leaf for insertion into bamboo. D) Inserting leaf and rice into bamboo section. E) Roasting bamboo joint and rice over an open fire. F) The finished product, once the bamboo is split open. Demonstrated by Amay Doyén.

[18] *Lekék* is a monocot with a supple leaf.

Social aspects of the Manobo economy

Kinship organization of economy

Decentralization

The intrusion of settlers and loggers has not only reduced the amount of land available to the Manobo. It has also created pressures which have forced the Manobo onto a trajectory of greater centralization in their own social organization. To understand that trajectory, however, it is useful to reconstruct as much as possible the character of pre-invasion social organization. Manobo society was, before settlers began to arrive, highly decentralized, as has been found to be the case among other pre-chiefdom horticultural groups in Southeast Asia and elsewhere organized into autonomous villages. As is true for many peoples practicing swidden agriculture, houses were widely separated or in small clusters; there were place names, but no villages. As for access to land, Manobo agriculture functioned in the context of a traditional usufruct system. By the ground rules of this system, the land was under the general control of the community. No individual household "owned" land in a modern sense. Individuals fully owned the produce of the fields which they planted. But to gain access to a particular plot, a man would ask the *datù*'s permission, which was freely given. Sulutan Edod Nayam's description of life at that time illustrates the situation well:

> We used to move around [farming in different places], but no longer. It used to be that when we wandered, we would sleep on the ground in the forest.
> [Sulutan Edod Nayam named several "clans," and said they were all united.] That is why we all live together [why our living place is not divided]. Before [the settlers] took our land, we here would go and farm on that man's land over there.[19] That's what happened to the land of Amay Dadù's father: it was taken by the "Christians" who "opened" Ketudak.[20]

---

[19] That is, they were free to farm on land that "belonged" to someone else. Each Manobo freely extended permission to other Manobo to farm on "his" land.

[20] Filipinos refer to those peoples heavily influenced by the Spanish as "Christian," *Cristiano*, or lowlander. The Manobo use the term *Bisayà*, referring to the Visayan islands in the central Philippines, from which most of the *Cristianos* have come. They use the term *Lenawen* to refer to the Maguindanao and Maranao, predominantly Muslim peoples who originally lived farther north. The term is derived from the word *lanaw*, which in Manobo and several other Philippine languages means "lake." The Maranao come from the region around Lake Lanao, considerably north of Manobo territory. In this book, I refer to the *Bisayà* as "settlers," and to the *Lenawen* as "Muslims" (as defined in the preface).

> In the past, before there were titles to land, if someone wanted
> to plant, they would not forbid him. They used large natural bound-
> aries (as mountains) to separate fields. When harvest time came, all
> [the relatives] would come to eat. That was how our ancestors did
> it. They cared for each other.

The preceding quote suggests that even rights to the produce were not jeal-
ously guarded. Individual households owned the produce which they planted
and harvested, but there were strong traditions—and associated social
pressures—to share this produce. In the case of land that had been "let go"
(allowed to return to forest), any bananas growing were harvested by whom-
ever was occupying the land, not by the one who planted them. However,
the person occupying the land might take some of the bananas to the one
who planted them. And, if the one who planted them happened to be passing
through, he might eat some of the bananas. If the one who planted a particular plant moved away, he no longer had any right to what he planted, but
he could ask for some. In short, not only were there no privatized property
rights over individual plots of ground, but even proprietary rights over the
crops that one planted were forfeited if the planter ceased to care for them.[21]

Personal kindred the basis of society

While many "traditional" societies studied by anthropologists have been
marked by a strong clan system, the Manobo, in keeping with other Philippine
peoples, reckon kinship bilaterally, through both the mother's and father's
side.[22] The group to which an individual is thereby related—his "personal
kindred"—is thus unique to himself and his full siblings, differing even from
the personal kindreds of his first cousins. Consequently, society was not automatically structured by kinship into large, cohesive groups. Kin were and are
vitally important, but it was the personal kindred that a person depended on,
not a cohesive clan.[23]

---

[21] The Western Bukidnon Manobo had similar practices toward land ownership
(Hires and Headland 1977).

[22] The society was traditionally patriarchal, but women could own property, and
property could be inherited through either side.

[23] The Manobo refer to the household by the term *gemalay*, meaning a man and
his wives and dependent children. (My informants said it would still be a single
gemalay if a man had 100 wives and they lived in 100 houses.) In its simplest form,
a *gemalay* is a couple and their children, plus any other dependents. If a married
child and his spouse are living with the child's parents, they are counted as part of
that *gemalay*. They become a separate *gemalay* when they live in their own house.
Likewise, if a couple or man or woman become too old to live independently, and
move in with an adult child, they become part of that child's *gemalay*. The term
malayan refers to a class of people having the same surname, but does not refer to
the cohesive unit anthropologists call a clan.

Establishment of marriage

We have already seen cooperation above the household level in the Manobo's sharing of meat obtained through hunting or trapping. Marriage provided another opportunity for supradomestic cooperation. Traditionally, marriage involved the exchange of brideprice (*songgud*), and was usually arranged. The account given by Amay Dadù of Elem is typical. His father chose a wife for him when he was about eleven years old and had no interest in marriage; he estimates his wife was about ten. They first had relations some four years later, when he was fifteen and she, fourteen. But, Amay Dadù felt he had no choice in the matter, because his father had paid the brideprice. The amount was substantial:

6 bridal canopies (*kulagbu*)
3 horses
5 large brass gongs (*selagi*)
15 swords (*sundang*)
50 ceramic bowls (of Chinese design or origin, with blue dragons painted on a white background)
13 *tabas* (weapons shaped similarly to the field knife, the *kelu*; see figure 2.2b)
"A little bit of money," estimated at P3,000.[24]

As the brideprice is typically far beyond the ability of a single individual to pay, assistance from relatives is vital. Assistance usually comes from the groom's father, uncles, and other close consanguineal kin. The groom in turn incurs an obligation to help those who helped him, often by helping their sons or younger male kin pay brideprice when the time comes. This reciprocity provided strong ties in the society. Amay Sumihay illustrated with his own story. In his case, he and wife chose each other, and their elders then helped make the marriage possible. He was nineteen years old at the time; she, sixteen. His father died when Amay Sumihay was only a few years old. However, when Amay Sumihay's uncle, Amay Egas, heard of his desire to marry, he called Amay Sumihay to him and told him he wanted to help out. Amay Egas paid the brideprice. Later, when Amay Sumihay received brideprice payment from his younger sister's marriage, he gave a carabao to Amay Egas.

The brideprice was often paid over a period of time, which also served to bind the society together. Traditionally, a newly married couple stayed

---

[24] Long conversations with Amay Dadù suggest that he was born about 1956. He would thus have been eleven years old in 1967, at which time the US dollar was equivalent to 3.90 Philippine pesos (Heston et al. 2006). P3,000 would have been equivalent to $769—at that time a tremendous amount of money. Five-, twenty-, and fifty-centavo paper notes were still in use. Currently, the smallest paper note is P20, and five-centavo coins are seldom seen.

with one of the couple's parents until they were old enough to earn a living on their own, at which point they were free to live wherever they chose. The usual choice was to live near the husband's parents. However, if the brideprice had not yet been paid, the couple was required to live with the wife's parents.

The Manobo say that the brideprice practice also helps to cement marriages together, as the brideprice is forfeited to the wife's family if the husband divorces her without cause, and must be returned to the husband's family if the wife divorces him without cause.

The Manobo society traditionally permitted polygyny. Due to the high brideprice, it was a mark of wealth, and greatly increased the size of the husband's "personal kindred," his network of consanguineal and affinal kin—an important step on the road to becoming a *datù*.

Property

While the Manobo were, in the past, concerned with usufruct rights rather than land ownership, they recognized rights to an active field. These were delineated by natural boundaries, such as mountain ridges and creeks, and as such were easily distinguished from one another. The practice of polygyny, however, requires more careful attention to boundaries. If a man has more than one wife, the wives divide the swidden, marking the boundary between the portions with cassava, or else have two separate fields. They keep their harvest separate from each other. However, even though they maintain separate food stores, the wives and their children may cook and eat together. Coffee[25] groves are owned by the couple, in the case of monogamous households, or by the wife in the case of polygynous households. In the case of polygynous households, the wife gets the profit, but also bears the cost of clearing around the trees. When the grove is cleared, her husband takes part in the work.

In the past, heritable property was limited to durable artifacts. The Manobo refer to such heirlooms as *pusakà, pegawà*, or *lalawan*. A *pusakà* is something durable which is passed on and retained by the heir throughout his life; he will not give it to another or sell it. It has the nature of a keepsake, of something which makes the user think of its previous owner. Potential *pusakà* include both traditional brideprice items (for example, large brass gongs, swords, *tabas,* and brass betel nut boxes and expensive, practical items used in everyday life (for example, field knives (*kelu*), cooking pots, and hammers). *Pusakà* are passed through the eldest living child, whether male or female. Should the child be too young to care for the

---

[25] Coffee is a cash crop and not a part of the Manobo's traditional agricultural system. The intrusion of cash into the Manobo economy and the adoption of cash crops are discussed in chapter 5.

heirloom when his parent dies, the item will be cared by the deceased's next oldest sibling until the heir is old enough to care it himself. If a person dies shortly before his rice is harvested, his survivors will harvest it and then sell one sack of rice to buy an heirloom item, such as a sword. The remainder of the rice is consumed by the deceased's survivors.

Political system

The Manobo have traditionally had leaders they call *datù*, quite similar in function to the leaders of other decentralized societies, such as the Big Men of traditional New Guinean societies (Pospisil 1978:47–52), and the *kéfédu-wan* of the Tiruray (Schlegel 1970:58–68). Unfortunately, the term *datù* can be misleading, as the same title is used by several predominantly Muslim peoples in the southern Philippines for far more powerful leaders. Prior to the arrival of settlers in Manobo territory, people lived in widely separated houses or in small clusters. Land use had to be cleared with the *datù*, but he readily gave his permission. His real work was conflict resolution.

The *datù* were arbitrators, who acted to keep aggrieved parties from taking their own revenge. *Datù* dealt with their own kin. They could negotiate a settlement between two parties if they were related to both of them.[26] In cases where the disputants are not (in their own judgment) closely related, each is represented by his own *datù*, who attempts to come to mutually acceptable terms with the opponent's *datù*. Sulutan Edod Nayam described how the *datù* dealt with killings:

> If someone was killed, the offender's *datù* would gather with several other *datù*, and each would contribute various items of *tamuk*, such as horses, carabao, swords, or large brass gongs. The group would then go secretly by night to the house of the kin of the one who had been killed, and stop within sight of it, where they would tether the animals and pile up the other items of *tamuk*. They would then leave without being detected. Once it became light outside, the people in the house would wake up and see the animals and go to investigate. When the murdered person's kin saw the *tamuk* they would weep, because they now knew they could not go on a revenge raid. If they went beyond the *tamuk* to take revenge, it indicated they were spurning the weregild, and the murderer's kin would then kill more of the victim's kin. After this, the offender's *datù* [singular] would summon the victim's *datù* [singular]. The offender's *datù* would bring a very large bowl and fill it with water. The water would be sprinkled over the *tamuk* and then the victim's kin would drink from the rest of the water. Unless this was done, the victim's kin would sicken and eventually their stomachs would

---

[26] Among the Manobo, "kin" are reckoned using a broad definition, as any two Manobo can usually find a consanguineal or affinal link between themselves.

burst and they would die. Performing the ritual would ensure that everyone was reconciled and that everything was fine.

Datù do not inherit their position, though they are frequently the sons of previous *datù*.[27,28] They are usually wealthier than their companions, and traditionally had a number of wives.[29] However, the key features were that they must be respected, able to speak well, and able to seek peace. When asked how someone became a *datù*, Marcelo Apang replied that they do so by being able to judge and to help, because of having good character, and because of being wise. Another respondent, Unik Atak, added that people become *datù* because they produce results. He also said that the *datù* never killed anyone; rather, if anyone was about to kill someone else, it was the *datù* who prevented it. That was is why the *datù* lived long. That was how Dakiyas (Unik's great-grandfather, so well respected that the Manobo refer to him as a *sulutan*) acted. He prevented murders. Consequently, all the Muslim *datù* liked him. Everyone who couldn't work went to him. All those who could not marry [that is, who couldn't afford to pay the brideprice] went to him and he enabled them to marry. *Datù* must act well toward everyone, including their wives and children and visitors.

The *datù* received substantial prestige for their work, but did not receive any direct payment for their efforts at the time. Datù Amay Ambing stressed that a *datù* paid settlements from his own *tamuk* (brideprice items). When I asked how a *datù* kept from depleting his supply of *tamuk*, Amay Ambing replied, "The *datù* spoke to his followers and urged them to help out the person [who was in trouble]. Everyone was healed because fury was avoided. The *datù* got what he asked for because it benefited the giver.[30] The givers therefore had a good heart to give."

Kalah's description of one incident illustrates the important role the *datù* played in averting violence. The conflict began when Amay Sintà cut off the arm of another, Amay Udes, in a fight:

---

[27] The term *datù* refers exclusively to males. The Manobo mention occasional cases of *booy*, a term they define as "*datù bayi*" (female *datù*). However, every time I have heard the term used, it has been in regard to a *datù*'s daughter; I have heard of no instance where a *booy* has settled a case or has negotiated in government matters with outsiders. It thus appears that while *booy* are respected, they seldom if ever exercise the same powers as a *datù*.

[28] Sulutan Edod Nayam, for instance, arbitrated disputes even before he received an official government title. He is not a *datù*'s son, but learned to arbitrate disputes by observing other *datù*.

[29] Amay Tiya, an old and respected *datù* in the village of Pokò Wayeg, had six wives. Datù Apang, ancestor of many of the people of Danu, had five (interview with Danu residents, January 2006). Datù Kalabaw, ancestor of many of those in the Elem area, had eight wives. Amay Tiya was still living in the first decade of this century. Datù Apang and Datù Kalabaw are grandfather to many people now in their late 50s, so would have been near the end of their lives somewhere around 1960.

[30] That is, the peace so obtained was to the giver's benefit.

Amay Sintà was a hothead. When I got [to Mayul, where the injured man's kin lived], they were getting ready for a raid....They had guns and daggers and spears and other weapons....I left my sheath and field knife behind, to show respect to those who were angry. When I got to Amay Sintà's house, I peered inside and spoke to him. I asked him to give me some betel nut chew, but he said he didn't have any lime [required as part of the chew], so I said never mind. [Kalah was trying to get Amay Sintà into a mood to negotiate.] Amay Tiig [a kinsman] and two others came....I gave a carabao and told Amay Sintà to lead it [to the injured man's kin], saying 'You're the one who committed the offense.' [The carabao] was small, but I exchanged it for a larger female with a settler. I also gave P700. Amay Tiya gave P300.

The Tiruray have had a similar leadership system, but distinguish between the offices of *kéféduwan* and *timuway*. Pastora Tita Cambo, of the village of Selumping, explained that the Tiruray *kéféduwan* is a term is equivalent to the Manobo *datù*. She likened the *kéféduwan* to an "attorney," but the *timuway* to a "judge." (The English words were given by Pastora Cambo.) If someone has a problem, he can go to the *timuway* with his complaint, and the *timuway* calls the *kéféduwan*. If the *kéféduwan*[31] are unable to settle the case, then it goes back to the *timuway*. The *timuway*, then, has the author-ity to make a decision, while the *kéféduwan* are arbitrators without binding authority. *Timuway* also serve as "senators," as "representatives" of their group to outside powers, also true of the Manobo *datù*. The Manobo term *datù* appears to encompass both *kéféduwan* and *timuway*: *datù* usually can-not impose their decisions, but may do so if the offender's behavior is so outrageous that the community will stand behind the imposition of unusual and extreme punishment, and the *datù* also represent those in their geo-graphic region to government officials or other *datù*.

The *datù* are to be distinguished from *alek*, a term which might be glossed as "war chief." *Datù* did not lead revenge raids (*pengayaw*), though might "bless" a raid.[32] A *datù* might also forbid a raid, in which case the raid was not made, as the *datù*'s word was higher than that of the *alek*. There was evidently no formal procedure to become an *alek*; all that was necessary was that one be hot-headed and a *tege-imatay* (one who often killed people). One example is that of Amay Sintà, mentioned earlier in the case of cutting off a man's arm. The Manobo speak poorly of a person who loses his temper, but in the case of the *alek* they have harnessed an otherwise destructive trait. Sulutan Edod Nayam described the *alek*'s function this way:

People who have children and are married should just concentrate on farming; they have no reason to do what is bad. That is what our elders taught us. But, if a person deliberately commits wrong, they

---

[31] In this instance, the word *kéféduwan* is plural. The Manobo and Tiruray languages do not have separate singular and plural forms for nouns.

[32] The English word "bless" was used by my informant.

would tell the *datù* about him, and the *datù* would tell them to kill the person. The *datù* would command his *alek*, who would set out with companions. When he drew near the wrong-doer, he wouldn't harm anyone else, just the wrong-doer. He would approach the wrong-doer's residence, and if there were others nearby, he would tell them to pass by and tell the wrong-doer that they had come to get him. The wrong-doer's companions wouldn't get in the way; they would go away. Then the *alek* and his companions would cut down the house[posts] and take apart the house and spear the wrong-doer. The wrong-doer's kin would not take offense at their kin's death.

Alternatively, the *datù* might punish a troublemaker by shutting him up in an unroofed pen for a few days, exposed to sun and rain. This was never fatal, though evidently quite uncomfortable, and likely humiliating as well.

Even now, when much of the *datù*'s traditional role has been taken over by the Philippine government, *antang* (customary settlements) can consume a considerable portion of a *datù*'s time. One may well wonder how they could afford to spare so much time from normal livelihood tasks. Sulutan Edod Nayam explained that he had his followers work in his field. He provided food, and they went and cleared his field. As he explained it, "My judging was like clearing a field. [The work of] *antang* cannot be neglected or our living would come apart."

Internal migration

The Manobo's oral history and the existence of traditional names in their language for places throughout their territory (table 2.1) attest to their long occupation of the region. However, the same history also shows considerable internal migration within the area. For example, the area of Elem, now the location of one of the largest Manobo villages, was once unoccupied; the Manobo lived many other places in their territory, but that particular area was settled during the lifetime of Kalabaw and his contemporaries. (This occurred four to five generations ago, depending on which person's genealogy is used.[33]) The areas of greatest Manobo population were once Miibu, Kanalan, and Kulaman. Binansél (later called Kapitan by settlers, and ancestor to the Kapitan "clan") lived in Kanalan but then migrated to Ketudak.[34] Dimaug (ancestor of another "clan" in Elem), along with a

---

[33] This was four generations ago, reckoned from Anggah's child to Datù Kalabaw, or five generations, reckoned from Jamin to Datù Kapitan, who was Kalabaw's contemporary. See "Genealogies" in appendix A.

[34] Settlers have changed the pronunciation and spelling of many places originally named by the Manobo. (Ketudak, called Keytodac by the settlers, in one such case.) In some cases, they have changed the name altogether. (Kulaman, for instance, was renamed Sen. Ninoy Aquino when it was declared a municipality.) In such cases I have generally used the Manobo name, in deference to the original inhabitants.

young relative of Nayam, began farming the area of Banigan. Kalabaw, Nayam, Lebeg, and Osong (ancestors of several "clans" in Elem) moved first to Banigan and later to Elem. The ancestors of the Opong "clan" likewise moved to Elem from Bugadu, near the Miles River. Individuals also moved from one area to another due to marriage. After Kalabaw moved to Elem, he heard of Binansél and went to Ketudak to meet him, after which the two "clans" began giving women to each other in marriage.

More recent history shows the Manobo's traditional readiness to welcome new-comers. While the Elem area was "opened" during the lifetimes of Kalabaw, Nayam, and Osong, the population in the area was evidently still low compared to what it is now. People in Elem say that Sulutan Amay Marcial was the real "first person" in the Elem area, who gave land to the Manobo who live there now. Sulutan Sabang explained, "At first there was just I. [Sulutan Edod Nayam] and I are the ones who opened the land here. If other [Manobo] came, we did not chase them away. We did this so that our people would grow in number." Sulutan Edod Nayam went on to explain, "We were all united; that is why our place is not divided [that is, why they all live together]. Before the settlers took our land, we here would go and farm on that man's land over there." Each Manobo freely extended permission to other Manobo to farm on "his" land.

Table 2.1. Place names

- Salangsang was named after the practice the *datù* had of beating a gong (*selagi*) to call other *datù* to a pre-arranged meeting. (Meetings were not held on a regular schedule, but the *datù* would arrange when they would next gather.) The gong's sound made the place *sangsangen*, from which word the place name "Selangsang" is derived. This was rendered "Salangsang" in the settlers' orthography. Dakiyas Belag, an important *datù* who was son of Belag and father of Dulin Belag, lived in Selangsang and was called Datù Selangsang, after his dwelling place.

- The Manobo do not remember living in Palimbang proper. However, they did live in Kibang (Winged Bean), which is now called Sarmiento Camp, in Bagumbayan.

- Dakel Kayu (Large Tree) is named after a large tree that was cut several years ago. There is another large tree of the same species growing there now, but the original tree was much larger. The old men believe that Kelisong was born before the original tree ever sprouted. Dakel Kayu has always been called by that name, from the earliest the old men can remember.

- Belag is buried in Keletalu Mountain. The *keletalu* is a large, green caterpillar with white bands, and the mountain looks something like a *keletalu*. Keletalu is in northwest *Barangay* Salangsang.

- Banigan, located near the Tran River, is named after a rock in an intermittent stream. The rock was where people gathered when they were prepared (*nebanig*).

- Ligoden was so named because it was avoided (*ligoden*) by people traveling in the area. Sigut Lebangen (Difficult Hips, so named because his hips were deformed) had a reputation for ferocity, so people traveling in the area detoured around his place.

- Ketudak has been known by that name since before one old informant, Amay Ibung, was born. Ketudak (Planting) was called that because of an epidemic which swept through the village many years ago. People were dying so quickly that the survivors could only dig graves so shallow that it seemed like planting yams.

- Tubak (Slide) is named after a large landslide which occurred there.

- Melawil is named after a person in the Manobo's traditional accounts. Their traditional stories relate that at one time the ocean flooded and was about to cover the entire earth. But, before it could do so, the Manobo, Melawil, climbed a sharp mountain and shouted over the water in a loud voice. His shout prevented the water from rising any higher, and it eventually receded. Melawil Mountain was the mountain he climbed.

- Kebuléng is named after a citrus tree that was once plentiful there.

- Pig-ubudan (Place for Seeking Palm Heart) Creek, near the village of Migàgà, is so called because it was a good place to obtain palm heart, valued as something to eat with rice or another staple.

- Tinapawan (Where the Snake was Prepared) is named after the time the Manobo killed and ate a large python there.

- Belatiken (Place of Many Spear Traps) was a good place to catch wild pigs with spear traps.

- Kulaman is named after a person who drowned in the river there.

Summary

The Manobo originally occupied a large area comprised mainly of highland valleys and slopes. The soil in the steeper areas was subject to erosion, but their traditional swidden system allowed the forest to regenerate, protecting the topsoil and suppressing weeds. It was an adequately productive system, amply providing for their physical needs. Yams, cassava, rice, and maize provided the majority of calories. Domestic animals were limited. They kept horses and carabao, but valued them for use in brideprice rather than as draft animals. Chickens were occasionally kept for eggs and meat.

The traditional Manobo society was loosely organized. It was supported by swidden agriculture, supplemented by hunting and gathering. With little trade with the outside world, the economy was essentially cashless. For particularly heavy tasks, such as clearing fields or harvesting crops, individuals mobilized additional labor through their kinship ties. However, as the Manobo kinship is bilateral (Elkins 1968), there were no true clans; each person relied on his personal kindred. Consequently, kinship did not supply the society with large, cohesive units, meaning there was little centralization above the household level. A few households might live near each other, but there were no large villages. Power was decentralized: the traditional leaders, the *datù*, had significant influence but little actual control. Their primary function was as arbitrators who sought to repair harmonious relations before those offended sought revenge. Only occasionally might a *datù* lead the community in imposing severe sanctions on a member who had repeatedly and intolerably violated community norms.

Land was considered to be common property, with usage rights allocated by the *datù*. Produce and game were the property of those who produced or caught it, but there was considerable sharing with relatives. Dependence on relatives extended to the payment of debts. The high brideprice, as well as large fines paid to right various offenses, necessitated assistance from relatives, thereby binding individuals together in a network of obligations.

Thus, traditional Manobo culture was well-adapted to their situation prior to the coming of intruders from outside. The livelihood system provided amply for their needs and was environmentally sustainable. Personal kinship ties supplied additional labor for heavy tasks, and the *datù* were frequently able to avert violence and restore social harmony. The culture possessed little centralization, but greater organization was unnecessary. That situation, though, would quickly change with the coming of settlers and other intruders from the outside world after the mid-twentieth century.

3

The Felling: Subjugation and Adaptation 1953–1974

The last chapter presented a reconstruction of Manobo life during the first half of the twentieth century, particularly their economic and social organization. This chapter documents the intrusion of the outside world. As noted in chapter 2, a society may be impacted by another society in one of three ways: it may 1) "disintegrate" (become less organized), by accepting a position of reduced ability to control its own affairs and resources, 2) "integrate" into the more powerful and organized society, either retaining its original organization or becoming more organized, or 3) fight back and develop greater complexity ("surgent evolution") (Adams 1977:398–402). The Manobo's response to the influx of settlers (as defined in the preface) after World War II demonstrates all three possibilities: subjugation, adaptation, and resistance. The account of the arrival of settlers and their impact on the Manobo is, of course, of great significance to the Manobo themselves. Yet, as we note the specific mechanisms by which the Manobo were impacted and responded, their account also sheds light on the plight and possibilities facing many other indigenous peoples whose homelands are being invaded.

The invasion: National scale

The isolation that characterized the earlier Manobo lifeways described in chapter 2 was not to last. The seeds of its demise were planted years

47

earlier but came to fruition after World War II. Like many countries, the accidents of history have left the Philippines a culturally divided nation. Islam was introduced to Mindanao in the late 1200s by Arab traders and had reached Manila by the time the Spanish conquered it in 1571 (Man 1990:21). However, the Spanish were able to establish control over much of the Philippines and held the archipelago as a colony until 1896, when the Philippines revolted. At the same time, Spain became embroiled in war with the United States. The Philippines declared its independence from Spain in 1898, but Spain, on its defeat by the US, ceded the Philippines to the States, and the US became the new colonial power.

American investors and wealthy Filipinos looked south to Mindanao as a new territory to exploit. It had mineral deposits, vast areas of forest, and a relatively low population density, suggesting the ready availability of land for plantations. Additionally, Luzon and the Visayas had large populations that lacked adequate land. The way for business investment was cleared by the extension of the Public Land Law to Muslim provinces in 1906. The law provided for the granting of title and had the stated intention of helping Muslims escape from serfdom, but also allowed newcomers to claim land at the locals' expense. Large rubber and peanut plantations, owned by individual Americans, soon arose. This was followed in 1913 by other laws encouraging migration to Mindanao (George 1980:108–109).

The Commonwealth government (1934–1941) accelerated migration. The government wanted to exploit the timber and agricultural potential of its southern territory. It was also concerned with forging a national identity. The Philippine population is comprised of 182 different language groups (Lewis et al. 2015b), and the mingling of settlers with each other and with the indigenous peoples of Mindanao would help to forge a more homogeneous population and thereby encourage national unity. In 1938, General Paulino Santos led a project to survey the Koronadal Valley for settlement; two years later, the Allah Valley was opened. Settlement continued at a high rate for many years; in the 1960s, fully 20 years after settlement began in the Allah Valley, as many as 3,200 people per week were arriving in Mindanao (George 1980:111–114).

The invasion: Local scale

To understand the impact of national policy on the local population, and their adaptation and response to the pressures this caused, we now turn to events as they unfolded at the local level. Interviews[1] with some of the older Manobo put a concrete face on otherwise abstract history. The genealogy in figure 3.1 may be helpful in following the account.

---

[1] The data for this chapter are taken from interviews with 54 informants (ten women and 44 men). Most of the interviews were taken from June 2005 through October 2006 and from September 1994 through September 1997.

The Manobo once occupied a wide area, encompassing that portion of Sultan Kudarat Province between the Celebes Sea and the mountains west of the Allah Valley, plus portions of southern Maguindanao Province and northwestern South Cotabato Province. Amay Tiya was not yet a teenager when he first saw Japanese and American planes fighting above Lebak. He is an old man now living in the village of Pokò Wayeg. He related that when he was still young, there were few or no "Christians" or "Muslims" in the Kalamansig area.[2] His father, Toel, lived in Ketudak, where he had become a *datù* due to his skill in conducting *antang* (conflict negotiations). Apparently outsiders considered him a leader among the Manobo, for when war broke out with the Japanese in World War II, Filipino soldiers sometimes stayed with Toel. One of their commanders, Lieutenant Reyes, was in charge of guarding Kalamansig, a place Amay Tiya became better acquainted with when his sister married a Manobo from that area, Bago Datù.

Arrival of settlers

At that time, Salangsang and Ketudak, in the mountains above Lebak, were occupied only by Manobo. Then, in 1959, an Ilocano[3] named Pedro Gabriel arrived. Some of the Manobo say he had been a leader in the Hukbalahap, a militant land-rights movement in Luzon that fought against the government. He asked the Manobo for permission to hunt around Ketudak, so they took him throughout the area. Gabriel returned with several other settlers and asked permission to live there. The Manobo, who had a different understanding of land ownership, allowed the settlers to live on their land, never imagining that the settlers might claim it as their own. A few years later, Gabriel called for the Manobo elders and requested them to "release" the land, and asked what they wanted to do. The elders replied that they would divide the land with the settlers. Gabriel, however, gave them a small payment of salt, dried fish, tobacco, kettles, and fermented fish; he then told them that Ketudak was no longer theirs, and told them to move to Selumping, where he said he would build them a school with a teacher. So, because there were now many settlers and the Manobo were afraid of them, the Manobo moved to Selumping, about six kilometers away. Once they had moved, Gabriel claimed their land as his own and sold it to other settlers.[4]

---

[2] Amay Tiya placed the coming of the Muslims to Lebak as occurring when Macapagal replaced Quirino as president of the Philippines in 1953. In reality, Ramon Magsaysay replaced Elpidio Quirino as president in 1953; Diosdado Macapagal was elected to the presidency in 1961. From comments made by acquaintances who live in Lebak, it seems there were Muslims in Lebak by the time that settlers from the northern and central Philippines arrived. Hence, Amay Tiya probably placed the year of their arrival correctly, though misidentified who it was that succeeded President Quirino.

[3] The Ilocanos are a mainstream Philippine people from the northern island of Luzon.

[4] The settlers' account, given in a typewritten history of the *barangay* authored by Barangay Secretary Benny Y. Castro (n.d.), differs somewhat on the details but accords on the essentials.

After the Manobo moved to Selumping, Muslims under the leadership of Datù Kimpay learned of their arrival and began "visiting" them. Datù Kimpay would come during rice harvest and ask for rice and horses, and even forced the Manobo to allow him to lie with their wives. The Manobo decided they could not live with this situation, so moved to Belitbit in Piyusù, and then to Bulaan. They had only a small area available to them in Bulaan, for there were already settlers there, so they moved again, to Ligoden. Ligoden, however, was under the control of Pedro Gabriel, now barrio captain of Ketudak. He forced the Manobo to carry out much manual labor—harvesting maize, digging a road that went nowhere, hauling sand, bamboo, and wood—without paying or feeding them. He also asked the Manobo for rice at harvest time. Faced with this oppression, some of the Manobo moved away, to Pokò Wayeg.

Settlers sometimes obtained land through deceit rather than force. One informant recalled the conversation his father and a settler leader had about the land in Neligsegan (now known as *Barangay* Bululawan, near Salangsang):

> [The official] said, "Brother, if it's all right with you, this place where your mother is buried, this Neligsegan—let's make it a *bar-rio*." So my father said, "What do you want to do, Brother?" [The official replied,] "If there come to be many houses in this *barrio*, we'll give you thirty pesos for each house every month." My father said, "If that's what you want to do, then all right, so long as it leads to good." But now, it's full of settlers, and we aren't there, where my father's mother is buried. We haven't gotten even a *ketep* [one-tenth of a peso, currently US$0.002]...He promised, but didn't fulfill his promise. Now we live in Migàgà.

Similar events transpired in Kulaman, to the east, where settlers accompanying a different settler also named Gabriel arrived. Gabriel gave the *datù* some dried fish in payment for the land he was taking and threatened to shoot them if they did not agree.

Events unfolded similarly in the Kalamansig area. Kambing, a man probably in his mid-40s at the time of writing, related the history of his ancestors who lived in that area (figure 3.1). He described Kalamansig as having neither Muslims nor settlers when Kamelen, six generations earlier, was alive. Three generations later, though, there was evidently some governmental presence: a Philippine politician had Pabelu's uncle kill a political opponent. When the government in turn killed Pabelu's uncle and arrested some of his relatives, Pabelu and his kin moved away.[5]

---

[5] It will be noted that the Manobo consistently chose to move away, avoiding conflict rather than fighting back. Part of this may be attributed to the perception that humans cannot be expected to keep their emotions in check, and must therefore be appeased, or conflict avoided (Schlegel 1970:29–30). However, their interactions with the newcomers gave them additional reasons. The Manobo had observed that

Kamelen

|

Bosoken

|

Buwaya

|

Pabelu

|

Mandung

|

Kaliyu

|

Kambing

Figure 3.1. Genealogy of Kambing.

Widening ethnic conflict

At the same time that the settlers were moving into Manobo territory, conflict was erupting between the settlers and the Muslims. The settlers were moving into Muslim territory, and the Muslims were moving into Tiruray[6] and Manobo land. In Bugadu, down in the Lebak plain, Muslims ambushed the Manobo and slowly took over their land. Farther north, in the province of Maguindanao, war broke out between the settlers and Muslims; the Tiruray were drawn in, sometimes as combatants, often as innocent victims. Many moved to Salangsang in 1964, along with a few settlers.

The year of 1964 was important for another reason: Magsaysay and Sons Company (M&S Co.) began logging operations in Gintales, in the Lebak plain. In 1969, the company built a road through Salangsang and Danu to Ketudak and began logging in the mountains. Significantly, the company at this point in history conducted itself well toward the Manobo there,

---

their own weapons were much less powerful than those of the settlers. Furthermore, they had observed that conflicts with settlers invariably led to the state's intervention on the settlers' side. These pragmatic considerations reinforced their prior cultural tendency to avoid conflict, leading them to move away whenever practical.

[6] The Tiruray are a people culturally similar to the Manobo, whose traditional territory adjoins the Manobo's to the north. The Tiruray orthography is almost identical to that of Manobo, except that Tiruray uses the letter *f* in place of the Manobo *p*, and the values of *e* and *é* are reversed. The Tiruray refer to themselves as Téduray, but are known as Tiruray in the literature.

consulting with them before undertaking projects and not taking any land by force.

The Manobo's situation took a new turn in the early 1970s with the outbreak of the Toothpick War. Conflict between the lowland settlers and Muslims had been building for decades. Like the Manobo, the Muslims understood land to belong to the community, not to individuals, and thus often failed to recognize titles as legitimate. Tension between the settlers and Muslims was compounded by the Muslim practice of collecting in-kind levies on farm produce, which the settlers considered to be extortion. The ill-will between settlers and Muslims was further exacerbated by the Bureau of Forestry's practice of including in logging concessions areas which Muslim communities had already planted coconuts and other trees (George 1980:115–116).

The violence heated up gradually. Tiruray militias had already driven Datù Kimpay from Selumping by 1970. More Tiruray moved from Upi to Selumping from 1971 through 1973, due to conflicts with the Muslims in Tiruray territory. Lowland settlers began to arrive in large numbers at the same time. In 1970, the lowlander Ilaga movement, led by Commander Toothpick[7], declared war on the Muslims, and the Muslims fought back (George 1980:143–148). The Manobo responded to the situation by attempting to drive the settlers from the Kulaman Valley.[8] This allied them in the settlers' eyes with the Muslims, even though they had suffered from Datù Kimpay's predations a short time earlier. At the same time, many of the Tiruray (George 1980:143–150), including relatives of those now living in Selumping, fought alongside the Ilaga, in protest against the various "contributions" that Muslim warlords had demanded from them in years past.

Direct involvement of the national government

This regional drama was complicated by wider events in the rest of the Philippines. Its long history as a colony had given rise to a small landed class and large lower class. The great economic difference inspired the Hukbalahap Rebellion of 1946–1954. The unrest was temporarily defused by land reforms initiated by then-Secretary of Defense, Ramon Magsaysay, in 1950. However, as the economic gap persisted, a Communist insurgency grew. With the Vietnam War still raging to the west and many Filipinos concerned about increasing unrest, President Ferdinand Marcos declared martial law in 1972.

The imposition of martial law further eroded the Manobo's already tenuous standing with the Philippine government, opening the door to grave abuse. In one instance, a Manobo man named Dayek was falsely accused

---

[7] He was so called because of his slender build.

[8] Significantly, this is the first time that the Manobo attempted to resist the settlers with violence.

of being a rebel. Government soldiers trampled and stabbed him and then buried him after he died. In another instance, a Manobo man was passing through Gintales when he saw soldiers there. Frightened of them, he ran away and climbed a mango tree to escape them. The soldiers surrounded the tree and shot him, killing him. In still another incident, soldiers seized two Manobo men, bound them, and loaded them into a dump truck to take to a place where they had already dug two graves. While the soldiers were driving them there, the Manobo cut through their bonds on a sharp edge in the truck and jumped out of the truck, rolling down a slope. The soldiers shot after them, but the men escaped unharmed. Filipinos have condemned martial law for the abuses it brought throughout the country, but it seems the government's low regard for non-mainstream Filipinos resulted in even worse abuses of the Manobo.

Transformations in the political system

The Manobo's contact with the Philippine state has produced mixed results. In the early stages of contact, Muslim leaders and the Philippine government seem to have extended a certain amount of respect toward the Manobo, and were responsible for conferring greater standing upon the *datù* they chose to interact with. This is reminiscent of Morton Fried's (1975:i) contention that many "tribes"—groups having minimal political and economic internal integration, and with apparent but relatively weak hierarchical leadership—are the product of a state engendering hierarchy within a group so that the state may better control it. Bago Datù (cf. p. 49), for instance, is said to have been highly regarded by both Muslims and settlers, and was recognized as a *datù* by both Muslim *datù* and the mayor of Lebak. However, later interaction with the settlers and their government undercut the *datù* system. We have already seen how the settlers and Muslims in Ketudak, Kulaman, and the Lebak plain wrested control over land from the *datù*. In addition, the imposition of an alternative judicial system further undermined the *datù*. Cases between the Manobo and settlers were settled by government-recognized officials, not by the *datù*. Even among the Manobo, if someone was unhappy with the settlement the *datù* negotiated, he could take his case to a government official, who might overrule the *datù*. The *datù* continue to hear and settle cases, but only as the lowest "court of law." In Adams' terminology, the *datù* have "integrated" into mainstream Philippine society, taking a subordinate (and somewhat reduced) position in the social structure. Sulutan Edod Nayam expresses the frustration of many Manobo with the result:

> Now it takes a long time to settle a case. When the military gets involved, they make an appointment to deal with the case weeks from now. But if it takes a long time, the victim's kin will kill [in revenge]. We are being destroyed because of the military. Before, if

> something bad was done, our ancestors would settle it by afternoon
> of the same day. There was no *capitan* then. *Barangay* captains take
> bribes and do not judge rightly, so the victim's kin kill in revenge. If
> we could return to our old way, there would be fewer people killed.

While the government has allowed the *datù* to function as petty judges,
it has placed all substantial authority in the hands of its own officials.[9]
In many places, this has resulted in parallel systems of authority. The
village of Danu, for instance, has had both *datù* and *sitio* leaders, but the
government interacts with the *sitio* leaders, ignoring the *datù*. *Sitio* and
barangay officials are elected. As the Manobo tend to live apart from the
settlers, Manobo villages often have predominantly Manobo officials, while
the *barangay*, which are larger and include many villages, are governed
by settlers or Muslims. A review of the officials of *Barangay* Ketudak, for
instance, shows that in the last fifty years, only one official—Agut Tilam
Kapitan, a member of the Rural Police during 1957–1966—has been Manobo.
One, the current *barangay* captain, has been Muslim; the remainder have
been settlers. While the Manobo have had little influence at the *barangay*
or municipal level, there is evidence that is changing: two of Salangsang's
seven *barangay* councilmen are Manobo. However, the Manobo continue
to be heavily underrepresented in the government bodies controlling their
territory.

Impact of a market economy

The arrival of settlers transformed not only the Manobo's political system,
but also their economic system, resulting not only in their adoption of a
cash economy, but also the perception of land as property, the explicit
recognition of productive resources (that is, acceptance of the concept of
capital), the sale and purchase of labor, and the adoption of many of the settlers' economic practices. With the loss of large portions of their land to the
settlers, many Manobo resorted to borrowing from settler lenders, resulting
in further loss of land.[10]

Property

In the traditional swidden system, individuals' fields were clearly distinguished by natural boundaries such as mountains, ridges, and rivers.

---

[9] The Tiruray similarly report that there are still *képéduwan* and *timuay*, but that
the government refers to them using its own titles of *lupon* (Tagalog for "arbitrator")
and "tribal leader".

[10] The other Manobo peoples of Mindanao have experienced similar changes from
the influx of settlers. Hires' and Headland's (1977) description of changes in the
Western Bukidnon Manobo people's agricultural practices is a well-documented
case.

Co-wives might divide a shared field by planting a border of cassava between their individual portions, but there was no need to mark permanent boundaries. Land was used, but not owned per se. With the coming of settlers, though, the Manobo have had to define land as property or risk losing access to it. They therefore have adopted the settlers' customs for marking possession, as by planting banana trees along the boundaries of their fields.

The government claims all land as its own unless it has been officially "released" for titling. As settlers have come in over the years, the government has gradually released areas of Manobo territory the settlers have occupied for titling, while land that is occupied by Manobo, or that settlers are currently expanding onto, remains classified as national forest. However, settlers readily buy and sell rights to occupy such untitlable land, and the local government considers such transactions legitimate. The Manobo have had to conform to government practice, and now treat land as alienable property, not only selling to and buying from settlers but from each other as well.

The intrusion of a cash economy has also affected how the Manobo regard forest products, once considered open-access resources. Informants regarded materials that are not planted or cared for (for example, rattan, deer, wild pigs, river fish, frogs, wild bamboo, and wild abaca) as available to everyone. Timber species are treated somewhat differently. If they occur in land controlled by the logging company they are considered off-limits. An individual may use a tree if it is on his own land. He may also allow another Manobo to use the tree if he does not need it himself, sometimes for free, and other times for a small fee based on the amount of lumber sawn.[11] Some plants that were previously wild are now being planted. *Apus*, a large bamboo used as building material, grows wild in some areas but is planted in Elem. One informant said he allows others to use his *apus* for free if he does not need it, but that some Manobo are charging P5 per stalk. A few people are trying to grow rattan. There are a few edible plants that grow as volunteers on unused farmland, such as *selawì*, a hairy leguminous vine producing a seed similar to the butter bean. The Manobo sometimes eat the beans during the weeks after the last harvests of rice and maize have been depleted and before the new crop starts to bear. Anyone may harvest *selawi* from anyone's land, though the land owner is usually told about it, after the fact.

The Manobo's recognition of land as property has led to the adoption of another practice from mainstream Philippine society: sharecropping. In the settlers' version there are three parties—crop-grower, land-owner, and carabao-owner—each of which gets one-third of the harvest. If the land-owner provides fertilizer for the crop, the crop-grower must return the

---

[11] That is, the tree owner may charge P1 per board-foot of lumber sawn. At the time of the interview (June 2005), lumber was selling for P6 per board-foot.

purchase price for the fertilizer when he harvests the crop. The Manobo allow some variations on this. One informant said that if the land-owner also provides use of a carabao, he is entitled to one-half of the harvest, rather than the usual two-thirds. Another informant allowed a relative to grow maize on some of his land, and also cleared the land of brush for planting; in return, the crop-grower gave him one-fifth of the harvest.

The Manobo have also adopted the settlers' practice of leasing animals. They distinguish between borrowing an animal for draft purposes (*kepesabà*, meaning "causing to be grasped") and borrowing to raise (*kesagud*). Carabao may be borrowed for draft purposes; pigs and chickens, to raise and slaughter. If a farmer borrows a carabao, he gives the animal's owner 40 percent of the harvest. If the borrowed carabao is bred and bears, the owner and borrower split the progeny.[12] The first goes to the borrower, the second to the owner, and so on. The split is supposed to be 50–50. So, if the animal bears only one offspring, the owner and borrower agree between them who will get the one offspring, and who will in turn be paid for his half of the offspring. The arrangement is somewhat different for animals raised for food. If a farmer borrows a sow to raise, the farmer and sow-owner divide the offspring evenly when they are weaned, and the sow is slaughtered and equally divided. In the case of raising a barrow, the animal is divided equally when slaughtered. The arrangement is similar for chickens, except that the hen is not slaughtered after raising a batch of chicks. Instead, if the hen's owner is generous, he will give the care-giver one of the chicks (to compensate for not getting one-half of the mother), after which the remaining chicks are divided equally between hen-owner and care-giver. The owner may then reclaim his hen when he desires, without any hard feelings on the part of the care-giver.

Along with the introduction of a cash economy has also come the opportunity to borrow money, either to meet cash needs or to purchase crop inputs. Unfortunately, the interest rates available to the Manobo are crippling. The most common rate is a flat 10 percent per month (that is, the interest on a loan of P1,000 is P100 per month until the debt is paid). If the borrower cannot repay, the lender demands collateral, usually a horse or carabao or land. If no collateral is available, the lender may have the borrower jailed. When seed is bought on credit, the buyer does not take out a loan per se, but instead pays a highly inflated price. However, if the buyer fails to pay for the seed at harvest, the debt immediately begins to accumulate interest. One farmer took two years to pay for seed, at the end of which he paid P20,000 for the seed and P40,000 for the accumulated interest.

---

[12] When animals are bred, the sire's owner is paid a stud fee. In the case of carabao, the bull's owner is paid P100 if and when the cow becomes visibly pregnant. In the case of pigs, the boar's owner is allowed to choose one piglet from the resulting litter.

Perhaps even more damaging has been the introduction of *kesandà*, roughly translated as "mortgage." A land-owner borrows a sum of money, in exchange for which he surrenders use of an area of land until the debt is paid. This differs from the Western practice of mortgage in that the borrower not only puts up his land as collateral, but loses use of the land until the debt is paid. Many borrowers find it hard to repay the debt, thereby forfeiting their land for less than if they had sold it outright. If the borrower takes a long time to redeem his land, the borrower and lender must agree on new terms for the loan. If they cannot agree, the case may be heard by the local *datù* or *purok* chairman. (*Purok* chairman is another term for *sitio* leader.) However, the creditor may simply take over the land, particularly if he can bribe the authorities. Land is also lost when creditors claim a wider area of land than the loan agreement specified. Informants gave one example from Belah (figure 3.2), in which a Manobo mortgaged two coffee groves in opposite corners of a large field to a settler. The creditor later claimed the transaction was for the entire field, and was not a mortgage but a sale. This is reportedly a frequent occurrence.

Horses and carabao may also be "mortgaged," but not pigs. The creditor gains use of the animal put up as collateral as a draft animal. If the animal cannot be used for draft purposes because of the agricultural season, the creditor demands a flat 10 percent interest per month, but keeps the animal as collateral.

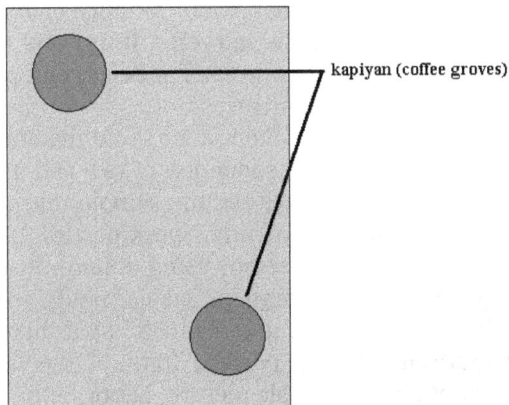

Figure 3.2. Mortgage of two coffee groves within a field in Belah.

Labor

The intrusion of a cash economy has also transformed labor practices. In the past, if household labor was insufficient, the Manobo would rely on cooperative work groups for help. If someone was clearing a field, for instance, he would ask several other men to help him. On the day they worked, he would feed the group, along with their wives and children. Or, if their families could not come, he would send food home with them. The farmer could expect those who helped him to call on him for help in their work, and he would readily reciprocate.

The Manobo still employ such arrangements, but with the coming of a cash economy they are also now selling and buying labor. Payment may be based on length of time worked, or may be a fixed amount to accomplish a given task. In the practice of *inagdaw* (meaning "by the day"), an individual receives an agreed-upon amount for a day's labor. Meals may be provided, or if not, then a higher wage is given. In the practice of *pakiyaw* (a word taken directly from Cebuano, spoken by many of the settlers), the laborer and the one hiring him agree on a price for the task. The laborer may then work quickly or slowly, depending on his desires, and may also hire other people to work alongside him. Farmers in the Elem area were paying P700 to prepare a hectare of land in mid-2005. If the land-owner fed the laborer, he paid less for the job, typically P600 or P500.

One practice which has changed little is that of recompensing harvest help. In the past, as now, those helping to harvest a crop are recompensed with an in-kind payment of a portion of what they harvest. What has changed, many informants say, is that the amount was not specified in the past: those helping harvest were allowed to take as much as they wanted. Many Manobo have now adopted the settlers' practice of *unus*, in which the laborer takes 20 percent of what he harvests. It appears that integration into a cash economy has resulted in greater precision on payment—a less personal and more formal arrangement.

Interviews of ten farmers in the Elem area show the Manobo's reliance on various sources of labor for the production of rice and maize (table 3.1). Some details are of special note. Within the sample taken, 34 percent of the labor was mobilized using cooperative work parties, 28 percent using unpaid household labor, and 15 percent using a share in the crop, while 12 percent was given without charge to a community leader[13] ("unpaid non-household labor"). Paid labor, and that provided through one-to-one reciprocation, comprised only 11 percent total of the labor mobilized. However, this does not give the whole picture. Labor for harvest was mobilized entirely by providing a share in the crop (80 percent of labor utilized) or through unpaid personal or family labor (the remaining 20 percent of labor utilized). Further, 100 percent of labor mobilized through giving a

---

[13] This is an important phenomenon, in that it shows the Manobo have a traditional mechanism that enables selected individuals to act on behalf of the group supporting them. At the same time, this source of labor is not available to most members of the community, so is not considered in my discussion of the Manobo's economic system.

share of the crop was utilized in harvesting. Most of the activities are carried out in temporarily short "bursts," but weeding stretches over a greater time. It is noteworthy that none of the labor required for that task was supplied by cooperative work parties or through reciprocal arrangements with peers. Most of the labor (65 percent) came from unpaid personal or family labor, with the vast majority of the remainder (30 percent) coming from paid labor. This suggests that the Manobo may tend to fall back on paid or family labor for "regular" tasks, but might favor utilizing cooperative labor (either parties or one-to-one arrangements) or a share in the product for "irregular" activities.[14]

---

[14] How the Manobo mobilize labor for farming may well have application to other goals they are pursuing, including the attainment of land rights. The data suggest that for activities of a regular nature, labor could probably be most dependably mobilized by payment of a wage or by dependence on volunteer labor (remunerated by increased social standing in the community). On the other hand, labor for occasional activities could probably be mobilized through cooperative work parties. Mobilization by giving a share could probably be used in other activities that directly result in a tangible product, but only in those cases.

This is consistent with what I have observed. Literacy classes (a regular and sustained activity) progressed well as long as there was outside funding. Classes of lesser duration (on farming techniques) have proceeded without remuneration. (Presumably, the increased standing in the community is sufficient remuneration compared to the opportunity cost of not being able to farm during that time.) Special activities like weeding the church grounds usually rely on someone calling a work party. Church funds are used to provide coffee for the participants, making the arrangement similar to the usual cooperative work party, where the crop owner provides food for those helping him.

Table 3.1. Sources of labor utilized in the production of rice and maize

Labor mobilization strategy	Value	Activity							
		Clearing	Burning	Plowing	Harrowing	Planting	Weeding	Harvest	Total
Cooperative work parties	Count	36		19		24			79
	% within strategy	45.6		24.1		30.4			100.0
	% within activity	70.6		51.4		35.3			33.5
Unpaid household labor	Count	6	6	11	6	16	13	9	67
	% within strategy	9.0	9.0	16.4	9.0	23.9	19.4	13.4	100.0
	% within activity	11.8	75.0	29.7	75.0	23.5	65.0	20.5	28.4
Laborers given portion of harvest	Count							35	35
	% within strategy							100.0	100.0
	% within activity							79.5	14.8
Unpaid non-household labor	Count		2	3	2	21	1		29
	% within strategy		6.9	10.3	6.9	72.4	3.4		100.0
	% within activity		25.0	8.1	25.0	30.9	5.0		12.3
Hired labor	Count	7				5	6		18
	% within strategy	38.9				27.8	33.3		100.0
	% within activity	13.7				7.4	30.0		7.6
Reciprocity between individuals	Count	2		4		2			8
	% within strategy	25.0		50.0		25.0			100.0
	% within activity	3.9		10.8		2.9			3.4
Total	Count	51	8	37	8	68	20	44	236
	% within strategy	21.6	3.4	15.7	3.4	28.8	8.5	18.6	100.0
	% within activity	100.0	100.0	100.0	100.0	100.0	100.0	100.0	100.0

Gender division of labor is likely similar to that before the advent of a cash economy, except that delineation of privileges and responsibilities may now be more explicit. Typically, the men clear the fields and the women plant. In polygynous households, the co-wives either have separate fields or mark the boundaries of their portion of a common field, but help each other plant. They keep their seed separate, though one wife may either give or lend seed to a co-wife. Each wife's harvest is kept separate from that of her co-wives. Coffee groves are owned by the couple, in the case of monogamous households, or by the wife in the case of polygynous households. In the case of polygynous households, the wife gets the profit; however, she bears the expense to have it weeded (that is, to have the weeds mown down with field knives). When the grove is weeded, her husband takes part in the work.

Incorporation into the market economy has transformed the Manobo's economic practices, destroying formerly effective CPR arrangements, converting land to alienable property, and monetizing labor. In the process, the Manobo's economic transactions with each other have become more impersonal and precise. It has also become possible to accumulate wealth, and to invest in productive resources. This is leading to the development of classes, not just of wealthy settler versus land-poor "native," but among the Manobo themselves. Some have much more than others, some Manobo working for other Manobo. Three brothers in Elem frequently work as carriers for others in the village, carrying grain from the *barangay* seat to the village, and coffee beans from the village to the *barangay* seat. In contrast, three other men in the village operate stores, buy coffee from other Manobo, and sell their own coffee and what they have bought in the *barangay* or municipal seat. They have become successful middlemen. Their families are frequently better dressed and in other ways appear more prosperous. Two of these men have considered buying a small grain mill, so that there would be a Manobo-owned mill in the village itself. This is evidence of an ability to accumulate wealth that was previously unknown, with the consequent widening of economic differences between villagers.

The Manobo have not demonstrated an awareness of class, perhaps because the phenomenon is still very new to them. However, they are quite aware that many Manobo are no longer as generous as in the past. As Sulutan Edod Nayam put it,

> Now, at this time, all of our Manobo kin are like the settlers. They don't give, because we don't have money, even though we are their Manobo kin. When they eat, they shut the door. That's what I put up with. When I eat, I refuse to shut the door, if it is my relative. If I have a little food, I refuse to make people pay for it. For example, if people come from Kulaman, I invite them. Where else would they eat if you don't invite them, for their place is far away. We don't forget the ways of our ancestors. Let's not take after the custom of the settlers.

Production system

Having considered the political and economic dimensions of the changes in Manobo society brought about by the influx of settlers, we will now turn to consider the impact of settlement on the Manobo's production practices. Much of what is described here will be familiar to those who have studied the impact of settlement on other indigenous peoples.

Perhaps the most obvious changes in the Manobo's economic system have been in area of clothing and tools. Access to a market economy has led to the complete replacement of traditional apparel by purchased clothing, the details of which were covered in chapter 2. The number of metal tools the Manobo use has also increased markedly over time. In the late 1930s and early 1940s, the Manobo had *kulut*, but no *kelu*. The *langgaman* (a blade held in the palm, used to cut the rice panicle from the stalk) had not yet arrived, nor had the hammer, or nails, or the grub hoe. *Kelu* were initially obtained in exchange for resin the Manobo collected from *tipedus* trees in the forest. It was only in the late 1950s to early 1960s that the Manobo acquired the knowledge of how to make metal tools themselves; Amay Empung was the first Manobo blacksmith in the region of Pokò Wayeg.[15]

The Manobo's incorporation into a market economy has also affected their methods of hunting and trapping. For those who can afford them, rifles and shotguns have replaced the spear for hunting pigs and deer, and air guns and rubber slingshots have replaced the bow and blowgun for hunting small game. The Manobo have also augmented the traditional spear trap and deadfall for catching wild pigs with the *timpung babuy* (pig bomb), a homemade grenade produced using the phosphor from commercially available kitchen matches. The maker wraps the *timpung* in bait and leaves it on a game trail he knows is frequented by wild pigs. When he hears the bomb explode, he goes looking for the unfortunate victim. Wild game is now scarce, likely due to the greater efficiency of the new methods, coupled with a much greater number of hunters and significantly less forest habitat.

Beyond the obvious changes in technology, the coming of settlers also profoundly changed the Manobo's relationship with the forest. Manobo now in their forties and fifties report that their ancestral territory was once covered in forest, but there are now few trees left on the land titled to settlers, and significant deforestation on untitled land as well. One resident of Elem summarized the change by noting that the great influx of settlers has made it impractical to let the forest regrow. The Manobo have much less

---

[15] Amay Tiya was about twelve years old when the Japanese and American planes were fighting in World War II, most likely near the end of the war, or about 1945. He was probably in his mid- to late twenties when Amay Empung began smithing, as he already had two wives. This would place the beginning of Amay Empung's smithing somewhere between 1958 and 1963.

land available to them than in the past, and if they attempt to let an area return to forest, settlers often claim the "abandoned" land.

Contact with outside technology and the need to make more intensive use of what land they have has also led to the adoption of new methods of farming. With the coming of the plow, the carabao, once used solely for brideprice, has become a draft animal as well. Many Manobo own carabao, and those who do not can frequently use one belonging to a kinsman, in exchange for a portion of the harvest. Plowed fields are planted to both upland (rainfed) rice and maize. The new technology impacts both income and the physical environment. In the swidden system, an area must be cleared at the beginning of dry season so that the vegetation will burn well before planting. With plowing, crops can be planted year round. The precipitation pattern and pest pressure limit rainfed rice to planting only one time per year in both swidden and plow-based agriculture, but maize can be planted up to three times per year in plowed fields. Farming therefore tends to be more profitable with adoption of the plow. Plowing also controls weeds without requiring regrowth of the forest, so land can be cropped year after year. This, too, contributes to potentially greater yields and profit. However, the soil is then exposed to rainfall continually, with no opportunity for regeneration. This is particularly significant in that the Manobo have been displaced from the more fertile flat land they prefer to farm onto much steeper land. Most of the fields I have observed have suffered extensive erosion. Older fields are eroded down to the subsoil, with the maize purple from phosphorous deficiency and stunted.

One of the most significant impacts of the Manobo's incorporation into a market economy has been their adoption of cash crops. Coffee and field corn account for much of the Manobo's cash income. The Manobo began growing coffee in the mid-1970s, after the close of the Toothpick War. Much of the crop is sold, either as green berries or as dried and hulled beans, but a small portion is retained for home consumption. The Manobo grow several varieties of field corn, which they call *sibù*, perhaps after the island of Cebu, from which many of the settlers came. The term applies to various hard-kernelled varieties, including *melalag* (called "yellow corn" by the settlers), *tanigib* (white kernels), "miracle" (also white), and "Cargill." Almost all of this crop is sold, as the Manobo prefer their traditional variety of maize for home consumption. In addition to the adoption of these new cash crops, contact with a market economy has led the Manobo to abandon crops that cannot be sold: grain sorghum, millet, and Job's tears are now seldom seen.

The Manobo continue to grow much of what they consume. Their preferred staple is rice, (though the annual harvest lasts only a few months) followed by their traditional variety of maize, then yams, then taro and cassava (ranked equally), and then bananas. They also eat yautia, the wild *bugan*, and field corn, but only if nothing else is available.

A few people raise cabbage, Chinese white cabbage, peanuts, and Irish potato, all of which were introduced by the settlers. A number of other crops provide variety to their diet. Many are traditional, including Chinese mustard, pigweed, sesame, tomatoes, and basil. A number of wild plants are also used, including *kolò* and *sikol* (the fruit and flower, respectively, of a wild ginger), vegetable fern, beggar's tick, *utan*, and *didip* (two species of wild greens).

Many peoples in the dominant Philippine society rely upon one particular staple year-round. In contrast, the Manobo's cropping system relies on several staples. Rice is harvested in August and September, but now that the Manobo have been forced to abandon the traditional swidden system, the harvest often does not last till the end of the year. Income from coffee, which is harvested November through January, may provide the means to buy rice. However, the price is dependent on the international market. Once coffee income is exhausted, *sasang bitil* (hunger season) begins, and the Manobo depend on root and tuber crops (cassava, yams, taro, and yautia) and greens. The lean season ends when the maize reaches boiling ear stage. The maize continues to be edible as roasting ears. (Both the traditional variety and field corn type may be eaten in these ways.) Eventually the maize hardens as it matures, and by July is eaten only as grits. A summary of the agricultural year is given in figure 3.3.

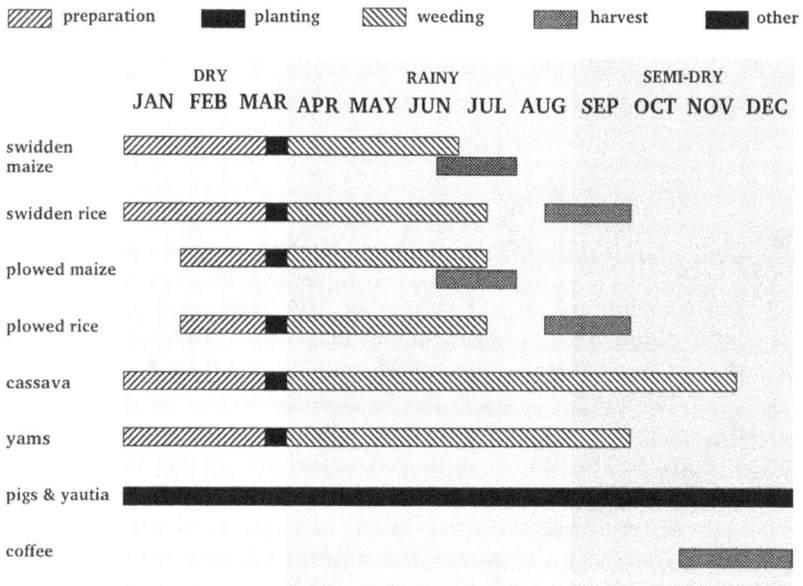

Figure 3.3. Agricultural year.

Impact of settlement on the biophysical environment

The influx of settlers has affected the biophysical environment, both directly and indirectly. The settlers practice sedentary agriculture, farming the same plot year after year.[16] This creates significantly more erosion than in the swidden system, as the forest, which would otherwise shield the soil and replenish both its organic matter and nutrient content, is not allowed to regenerate. Consequently, yields decline from year to year. Settlers have turned to chemical fertilizer in an effort to counteract losses in yield, but the use of inorganic nutrients has not been able to compensate for the loss in soil quality.[17]

The Manobo have been forced into adopting sedentary agriculture so that they do not lose "abandoned" land to the settlers, a change which has increased erosion on the land they farm. The switch to sedentary agriculture, coupled with the much greater number of people now living in the Manobo's homeland, has decreased the area occupied by forest. The loss of habitat, accompanied by a much greater population of people who are hunting and the use of more efficient weapons, has resulted in a marked decrease in wildlife.

The arrival of settlers and logging machinery has also introduced new weed species. One species, a fast-growing vine, has become a serious pest in coffee groves. One informant linked the new weeds to the construction of roads into the area, conjecturing that the bulldozers had brought in seeds and vegetative material on their treads.

In short, the intrusion of settlers and logging companies has resulted in numerous deleterious effects upon the environment: loss of forest cover, loss of habitat and the wildlife it supports, soil erosion, decrease in soil fertility, and the introduction of new weeds.

Summary

Some of the changes recorded in this chapter (summarized in table 3.2) may conceivably have occurred without the tripartite invasion discussed

---

[16] Unfortunately, this is *not* a sustainable system. The settlers cultivate the land using much the same system that they have used in the relatively flat lowlands, but that system is not suited to the pronounced slopes found in Manobo territory. Perhaps most of the land farmed by settlers has lost its A horizon, and many plots have eroded down to orange clay subsoil. Some conservation measures could halt the erosion.

[17] Recently, many farmers in the area (both *Bisayà* and Manobo) have lost their land to the merchants selling fertilizer. Farmers frequently buy fertilizer on credit and are charged high interest rates by the merchants. When yield increases from the fertilizer produce less additional income than the cost of the fertilizer and the loan payments, farmers forfeit their land to the seller. Informants report that most of the people in two villages near Elem no longer own land, and work as day laborers for the merchant they lost their land to.

here—settlers, loggers, and government agencies. Esther Boserup (1965) and others have shown that internal population growth can trigger changes in land tenure and agricultural technology, and societies may integrate into external markets without a violent invasion. But however much the Manobo's own population may have been increasing, the area's population clearly exploded with the arrival of settlers, far outstripping the effect of any indigenous population growth. The history of the region shows that the Manobo's population was not expanding significantly prior to the intrusion. Encouraged by the government to move to the "unoccupied territory" of Mindanao, settlers poured into Manobo territory after World War II and, with the state's complicity, forced the Manobo off their land through violence, threat, and deceit. The subsequent imposition of central state authority severely undercut the *datù* system, including the Manobo's provisions for managing land and forest and their mechanisms for resolving conflict and upholding the public peace. In addition to direct action against the Manobo's political system, the government was also instrumental in the Manobo's incorporation into a market economy in an underprivileged position. The settlers' introduction of the practice of mortgage, coupled with crippling interest rates, has resulted in many Manobo losing their land. Without the central government's involvement, settlers who made loans would have had to simply write off defaulted payments. Other settlers would then have refused to provide credit, and some or all of the Manobo would have lost their buying privileges. With government backing, though, lenders could press their claims for payment. However, while the government backed settlers' claims, it was slow to protect the Manobo's rights. In cases where settlers seized Manobo land through force or fraud, the Manobo could seldom receive a hearing from the settler-controlled local government.

While the Manobo suffered great setbacks from the incursion of settlers and loggers, and of the state that facilitated their penetration of Manobo territory, the Manobo have also adapted to the new political and economic system. They have adopted new crops that enable them to more readily compete with their new neighbors, and a few have become successful middlemen. The government continues to bypass the *datù*, but the Manobo are receiving increasing attention from politicians and government officials, and often now have their own government-sanctioned officials at the village level.

Table 3.2. Summary of effects of settlement on Manobo society

Domain	Arrangement in traditional society	After arrival of settlers and loggers
Political	Conflicts settled by *datù*	Conflicts settled by local government officials *Datù* bypassed Limited hearing of Manobo grievances by local government Settlement of grievances, when it occurs, is slow
Land	Managed as common property Emphasis on usufruct rights rather than on land per se Boundaries marked by geographical features Access controlled by the *datù*	Abrogation of common property regime Land claimed as private property by settlers, controlled as public property by loggers Land rights asserted by planting of conspicuous borders Widespread disregard for individual Manobo's property claims Land now sold, even between Manobo Land now considered collateral for debts
Labor	Routine labor supplied within household Greater labor needs supplied by reciprocation between kin	Partial replacement of reciprocation by wage labor Introduction of share-cropping Emergence of classes (settlers employing Manobo, as well as more prosperous Manobo employing poorer Manobo)
Exchange	Marked sharing of hunt catches and crops	Less sharing and more sale, both to outsiders and between Manobo More precise reckoning of debts
Agricultural system	Swidden agriculture	Sedentary agriculture Adoption of cash crops, and abandonment of crops lacking market value Considerable loss of forest Significant erosion and loss of soil fertility Introduction of weeds and insect pests Greater hunger than in past[a]

[a] Informants describe a steady decrease in yields over several years. Older informants report that the rice crop once provided food throughout the year. By 1984, most households were using up their rice within six months of harvest. Since 1997, many informants report they harvest only as much rice grain as they plant.

4

Seeds: Foundations for Resistance 1975–1988

The changes described in the last chapter will not surprise readers familiar with parallel situations in other cultures. The Manobo have experienced a situation common to many other indigenous peoples, in which the national government disregards their claims to the land, assumes control of their traditional territory, and opens the land and its resources to expropriation and exploitation by settlers (as defined in the preface) and corporations. Richard Adams (1977:398–402) points out that such external forces can produce one of three results in a society: 1) the society may disintegrate, decreasing in internal structure as a result of its decision-making powers being usurped by the intruding society; 2) it may integrate into the intruding society, increasing in internal structure as it is incorporated into the dominant society's political system; or 3) it may "surge," increasing in internal structure and, with the consequent increase in political and economic power, effectively resist incorporation into the intruding society. In their response to outside forces, the Manobo have, at one time or another, utilized all three of these options. We have traced how the Philippine government's promotion of transmigration and the consequent influx of settlers after World War II resulted in the "disintegration" of Manobo society, at the same time giving rise to economic adaptations at the household level. In the next period of their history, the Manobo experienced additional assaults on their society, but also began developing civil associations that would become the foundation for organized resistance to invasive forces originating from other sectors of Philippine society.

Disintegration

The arrival of the Magsaysay and Sons logging company (M&S Co.) in 1964 seemed to be a harmless matter, as the company under its original management acted in a manner that the Manobo interpreted as responsible.[1] The company began building a road from Lebak to the forested mountains farther inland. In 1966, the road reached Kiwag, a well-watered site that was home to about twenty Manobo families. (Kiwag is on the road between Salangsang and Danu). M&S Co. asked the Manobo for permission to establish a tree nursery there, and the Manobo's leader, Datù Ampuan, allowed them the use of one hectare of land for that purpose. At the same time, Datù Ampuan's people became concerned about the arrival of settlers in Danu, so some of them moved there to prevent the settlers from taking over their land. It appears the Manobo realized the settlers would recognize neither their traditional CPR arrangement nor their *datù*'s authority. They therefore asserted their rights to the land by making their presence obvious. Their efforts were partially successful, as only some of the land was seized by settlers. In Adams' (1977) terminology (cf. p. 15), the Manobo were "integrating" into the dominant Philippine society, in the process developing greater internal organization (for example, moving to Danu as a group to defend their claims) and accommodating themselves to the settlers' practices.

Whatever progress they made in adapting to the settlers, though, was dealt a setback in the mid-1970s when M&S Co. was purchased by Victor Consuji and came under new management. The move to new management was a momentous change. One of Consuji's first actions was to drive the Manobo out of Kiwag, so that he could establish a large nursery there. One informant's description of the company's new attitude was pointed: "Magsaysay was kind-hearted, but Consuji drove us out." A second incident a few years later, in 1978 or 1979, deepened the Manobo's distrust.[2] The Manobo assert that the logging company wanted their land in the several villages west of Kulaman: Siwal, Batasan, Ludù, Kenalan, Tinapawan, and Tubak. What is known is that the company told the Manobo in those places that they could load their maize onto a company truck to sell in Lebak. The road was rough and transportation limited, so several of the Manobo accepted the offer and boarded the truck with their maize. Significantly, no settlers (except for the driver, a company employee) boarded the truck with them. As the truck approached a steeper portion of the road, the driver opened his door and drove with it ajar. A short time later, the truck veered off the road and over a steep embankment. The driver jumped to safety, but

---

[1] The data used in this chapter were taken from interviews and meetings with land rights leaders, *datù*, pastors, residents of Elem and Danu, and colleagues. Most interviews occurred between June 2005 and October 2006.

[2] This incident was related to me by land rights leaders on two separate occasions, in 1998 and 2006.

twenty-four Manobo were killed, while another twenty-four were injured and taken to a hospital in Lebak. The company claimed the disaster was an accident, but the Manobo consider it a deliberate attempt to demoralize them and convince them to desert their land.

The company took several measures to protect its financial interests in timber. In the first place, the company asserted outright armed control over the forests. M&S Co. maintained (and still maintains) its own armed security force, what Filipinos call a "private army."[3] With this armed presence, company management was then able to impose and enforce restrictions against traditional agrarian practices that might have reduced its profits from timber. Concerned that fire might damage the timber they wished to remove or the trees they were planting, the company forbade the Manobo from practicing their traditional swidden farming system and threatened them with violence if they did so. This was a major challenge both to traditional property rights and traditional land use practices. It was an assault upon the Manobo's traditional management of the forest as a CPR. It was also an assault on a major component of their traditional agricultural technology, the felling of trees and the burning of desiccated plant debris. These processes have been documented in other settings as well where a government overrules local control of resources in order to allow their exploitation by outsiders via concessions of one type or another.[4] The enforcement of the new proprietary arrangements is then left to the concessionaire; the presence of armed guards of corporate beneficiaries has been documented in other parts of the world and at other points in history.

A further parallel effect has also occurred among the Manobo. As has been found in other instances, government interference with the local exercise of common property management can trigger off deterioration of the local natural resource base. This has happened through two analytically distinct mechanisms. The first is demographic. The presence of settlers, by reducing the amount of land available to Manobo, had created economic pressure on the Manobo to keep land in production, rather than allowing it to regenerate under forest fallow.[5] This is an instance of the famous

---

[3] When I speak of events in the present tense, I am referring to the first decade of the 21st century.

[4] One example is the case of the Cree Amerindians of northern Canada, who treated the beaver populations in their area as a common-pool resource. In the late 1920s and early 1930s, construction of a railway made the southern portion of their territory accessible to non-indigenous trappers. The Cree were not allowed to limit trapping by the outsiders, who heavily depleted the beaver population. When the beaver were reduced below profitable levels the outsiders moved on, and the Cree, this time with government backing, reestablished their traditional CPR system. Beaver populations recovered within ten to twenty years, depending on the particular location (Berkes 1989a:83).

[5] The settlers and Muslims rely upon on plow-based sedentary agriculture. Once they begin farming an area, they never let it revert to forest, and seldom allow it to have any fallow period.

and now classic analysis of Boserup (1965) concerning the shortening of fallow caused by a deteriorating person/land ratio. In this case, however, the demographically generated stress comes not from internal population growth but from the intrusion of outsiders.

The second mechanism was more direct: armed threats against traditional practices. Under its new management, M&S Co. threatened physical violence against the Manobo if they followed their traditional swidden agriculture practices.[6] At first glance a common sense reaction might predict a decline of destructive practices as a result of these prohibitions backed by weaponry. The prohibition of tree cutting and burning, whatever its motive, would seem to be a benign measure from the point of view of the environment. Here common sense is overridden, however, by ethnographic facts. This new factor of prohibitions enforced by weaponry paradoxically and unfortunately led to more serious erosion. Farmers of all ethnic backgrounds—Manobo, Tiruray, settlers, and Muslims—now regularly cultivate the steep slopes year after year, slopes that were formerly left virtually untouched. As the red clay subsoil on these particularly vulnerable slopes is exposed, crop yields are greatly depressed. In short, both the intrusion of settlers eager to claim land not under visible use, and the imposition of armed prohibitions against cutting and burning, sabotaged the traditional practice of allowing the soil to rest and regenerate under forest fallow.

Use of violence and the threat of violence by settlers, military, and company had sabotaged the Manobo's traditional forest and land management systems. But it also greatly disrupted their political and justice systems as well. The process converted the Manobo from the anthropological status of autonomous tribal cultivators to that of peasants—rural cultivators whose institutions had been supplanted by a central power, living on land they no longer controlled. In Richard Adams' (1988:398–404) terms, Manobo society had "disintegrated": as the Manobo lost power, their political structure fell apart and they were incorporated into the dominant society's power structure. These transformations in the context of political power triggered off simultaneous adaptations in the realm of land tenure and land use, as the Manobo were forced into a rapid shift toward sedentary agriculture and into a new property regime in which land was treated as personal and alienable property. These shifts in land tenure and land use occurred in the context of increasing levels of political subjugation.

---

[6] It should be noted that the company has also acted against settlers and Muslims in the area, though not nearly so often as against the Manobo or Tiruray. Informants related that in or about 1995, company security personnel destroyed *Bisayà* houses in Tibengtibeng, Sabanal, and Ludù. In the Ludù incident, the guards cut down the houses while their residents were taking refuge inside. Company security personnel also took chainsaws, rifles, and carabao from Muslims living near Ludù, but returned them after negotiations.

Foundations for resistance

Developments in Kalamansig

But the transformations and adaptations did not occur without resistance on the part of the Manobo. To understand this resistance we have to turn back the clock to pick up a strand of the Manobo's history that we have not yet discussed. World War II and the decades afterwards had brought the intrusion of the Philippine government, the settlers it encouraged to move from the northern and central islands, Muslim settlers, and M&S Company. However, the new political order also made possible the arrival of non-governmental organizations. In 1953, Philippine President Ramon Magsaysay invited the Summer Institute of Linguistics (now known as SIL International) to conduct linguistic research into the minority languages of the Philippines, translate literature into those languages, and promote vernacular literacy. As a result, SIL members Harland and Marie Kerr began work among the Manobo in 1955. The Kerrs were with the Manobo for only two years when they were reassigned to Papua New Guinea, but during that time they made substantial progress in learning the Manobo language. (Harland Kerr's (1988b) description of Manobo grammar remains an accurate and helpful introduction to the language.) Tom and Elnore Lyman took the Kerrs' place in 1957.

One item the Kerrs and Lymans began translating was the New Testament. In the process, some of the Manobo came to see the Creator in their traditional accounts as identical to the God of the New Testament. Among them were Ansen Utub and Pidal Utub, brothers who lived in the southern part of Kalamansig municipality. Ansen and Pidal adopted Christianity and convinced some of their kin to do the same, giving birth to a small but growing Manobo church. The church was initially led by Ansen. When he died a few years later (apparently of cholera), the leadership was taken up by Pidal, who was recognized not only as *pastol* (Christian pastor) of the community, but also as *datù* (traditional secular tribal leader).

The group originally lived in a village named Kepisek, but when settlers began moving in and taking over their land, they moved to a new site named Sangay. Clay and Helen Johnston took up residence near the group when they arrived in 1963 to continue SIL's earlier work with the Manobo. Ross and Ellen Errington joined the team in 1976, but took a location somewhat to the north, in Limulan.

By this time, the Manobo who had relocated to Sangay were again having trouble with the arrival of yet more settlers, and asked the Johnstons for advice on how to respond. The Johnstons and Erringtons in effect suggested flight rather than resistance, recommending that the Manobo consider settling in some place where there were no settlers nearby. Following these recommendations, Datù Pidal began looking for a place where he and his people could move. He made contact with another *datù*, Nonoy "Asuwang" Tumanday, who lived in the mountains above Kalamansig in a place called Belanga. Asuwang had also adopted Christianity and invited Pidal and his group to settle in Belanga, which they did in 1980. Belanga was thus essentially a religious colony, a feature which would prove significant in its later development.

In response to a request from the group, Ross and Ellen Errington recruited two women belonging to the Translators Association of the Philippines (TAP) to take up residence in Belanga and introduce literacy and health care. Beth and Pacita Lábaro, both nurses, moved to Belanga in 1982 and began training Manobo health workers and literacy teachers. Beth Lábaro later left, to be replaced by literacy specialist Mila Cagape in 1985. TAP also assigned workers to a location further east in Manobo territory in 1983, when Leoninda Guil-an Apang and Melita Bawaan took up residence in Kelusoy. Working together, these TAP and SIL personnel trained a large number of health workers and literacy teachers. They coordinated with the Philippine state, introducing those they trained to counterparts in government health and education offices. As a result of this contact with and support by an external NGO (see chapter 5, footnote 6), the health workers and literacy teachers gained both respect from the government and enhanced standing within their communities. One example of the new respect they gained is the clinic in Belanga, which was built in 1985 by a settler *barangay* councilor. The training of health workers also produced physical benefits, as in Belanga's initiation of vaccinations in 1986. Pacita Lábaro arranged for them immediately after a measles epidemic. The medicine came from Dr. Salcedo in the Kalamansig government, while the health workers administered the immunizations. Vaccinations for measles, DPT, tetanus, and polio, for children and pregnant women, have continued to the present. But quite apart from these material benefits, a new form of social organization was emerging that would begin to function in ways unanticipated by the SIL and TAP personnel who had introduced it.

Developments in Lebak

Events in the Kalamansig area became interwoven with those in Lebak. The movement of Tiruray and settlers into Salangsang in the 1970s (p. 51) was displacing the original Manobo inhabitants from their land. The Manobo in turn moved to Leman and then, in the late 1970s, to Elem. Manobo Christians from Limulan visited Elem in 1983 and explained the basics of Christianity to the people there. They visited Danu as well. They were received well in both places, and over a period of months several Manobo accepted Christianity, including Amay Bata, the *datù* of Danu, and Amay Luni Belag, a leader in Elem.

During this same period of time, settlers had increased in Limulan, where SIL members Ross and Ellen Errington had taken up residence; by 1983, there were very few Manobo remaining there. The men who had visited Elem suggested that the Erringtons move there. Taking their advice, the Erringtons built a house there in 1986, and visited several times beforehand.

While this was going on, the Manobo continued to contend with the increasing number of settlers. One locus of conflict was Ligoden, east of Ketudak. One of the men there, Mariano Capitan, heard about the church in Elem and visited there to investigate what the church was teaching. Mariano had learned to read in a government school, so Ross Errington invited him to read the portions of the New Testament he had translated. Mariano found the words to be *mengenaw* (cool and pleasant), and to fit well with the turmoil he was experiencing in Ligoden. He accepted Christianity and returned to Ligoden to share his new religion with relatives there. He was not initially well-received. However, Mariano found that Christianity gave him the confidence to resist the settlers who were oppressing the Manobo:

> I read God's words. It was like they were cool, like shade. There was nothing hot in [them]. I kept on reading...I carried God's Word back and taught it in church. That's where I had trouble...All of the *datù* were against me...including the *barangay* captain...But because God's Word was good, I kept on...[The time came that] my relatives decided to accept what RDB [a high official in M&S Co.] was teaching...they all agreed [to the lumber company's proposal to take over and plant the Manobo's land to trees, which the Manobo would then tend for wages], because it would be easy to get food that way...But I said that the [company's] proposal didn't make sense to me, so I couldn't agree. They said that my house lot would be planted to trees, but I said, 'Never mind. My eyes have been opened because of God's Word. Look at the birds. They don't have a place to store rice...But God takes care of them...Even if I don't have a place to make a living, God will keep me alive.' The *barangay* captain almost lashed out at me...But soldiers arrived and pointed their guns at him.[7] Thanks! Because that was due to God's help. And we're here [alive].

Mariano's relatives eventually came to accept Christianity, and a church was established in Ligoden.

One may posit that the Manobo were motivated to adopt Christianity because of the material and political benefits they perceived it would bring. However, such an interpretation represents an imposition of Western cultural categories on the Manobo. Like many indigenous peoples, the Manobo have traditionally regarded religion to concern this life as least as much as the next. The *beliyan* (shamans) concerned themselves primarily with healing, not with teaching matters of faith or conduct that would determine

---

[7] Government soldiers who were not under the *barangay* captain's command forced the *barangay* captain to back down and kept him from harming Mariano.

an individual's fate in the afterlife. When moral principles were explicitly taught it was frequently by the *datù*, the political leaders, in the context of resolving disputes; moral conduct was concerned more with maintaining harmony in society than with guaranteeing an individual's fate after death. The accounts given by my informants indicate that pastors were involved in addressing land rights from the very beginning. Ansun and Pidal, two of the very first to adopt Christianity, were the spiritual and political leaders of the community that migrated to Belanga. They preached, prayed for the sick, settled disputes, and led their people in dealing with conflicts with the settlers and loggers. When the Manobo converted to Christianity, it appears that they retained their traditional understanding of religion, and considered it appropriate for their new spiritual leaders to be concerned about matters of this world as well as the next.[8]

Emergence of the Association of Manobo Bible Churches, Inc.

By 1988, there were 75 Manobo churches, all led and taught by Manobo pastors who were using those portions of the New Testament that had been translated into Manobo. As the number of churches grew, the pastors became increasingly aware of their need for the Manobo churches to be recognized as legitimate by the government and by mainstream Philippine society. Part of the reason was to satisfy the demand of mainstream Philippine society for credentials; as in the United States and most places in the "modern" world, those who occupy positions of authority are expected to have formal education and official documents to attest to their position. Another reason was the presence in the Philippines of militaristic cults, militias that relied on amulets to protect their members from harm. The Tadtad (so called from a word in the Cebuano language spoken by many settlers meaning "to chop," due to cult members' attacks on their enemies), comprised mostly of settlers, were known to be active in the area. Apparently the government was concerned that similar movements might become established among the indigenous peoples, evidenced by one Tiruray informant's report that the government had suppressed their traditional religious gatherings because of fear that the gatherings would lead the Tiruray to kill people. In order to become an officially recognized religious organization, the Manobo churches applied to the Philippine Securities and Exchange Commission and became a legally recognized corporation in 1988.

---

[8] It is noteworthy that this involvement of religious leaders in political issues is hardly limited to the Manobo. The social networks embedded in religious associations have been called on to mobilize political action in a number of well-known instances, including the African-American civil rights movement in the US, Liberation Theology in Latin America, the Protestant Reformation, the American Revolution, and the now very high-profile role that Islam is taking in politics from northern Africa to Indonesia.

The Association of Manobo Bible Churches, Inc. (AMBCI), continued to expand. The usual process was that a Manobo community heard about the church and its literacy and health work in one village and asked the AMBCI to send them a pastor, literacy teacher, and health worker. As a church was established in that village and began health and literacy work, new villages heard about it and issued their own invitations. The AMBCI has now grown to 114 member churches.

The AMBCI's literacy and health programs

The Manobo's traditional view that religion concerns current life as much as the afterlife led to ready adoption by the emerging church of the social welfare functions of providing health care and teaching literacy. Examination of the workings of the literacy and health programs provides additional insight into the network of civil associations that was emerging, associations that would eventually provide a foundation for the pursuit of secure land tenure. One point is that a number of Manobo adults gained the ability to read through the literacy program. In the last six years alone, the program has held classes in 28 villages, graduating 641 in basic literacy and 1208 in advanced literacy. Annual figures in basic literacy were higher in earlier years, when more of the adult population could not read. Informants in Belanga estimated that the literacy rate in that area for individuals from 15 through 50 years of age is about 80%. The literacy rate in the Elem area is probably similar. A group of middle-aged women (most pre-menopausal, and all with children) there reported that all of them can read; all but one of their spouses could as well. They further reported that few of the women in Elem cannot read, and that almost all of the men in the church there are literate.

A second point is that the literacy program was dependent on outside funding,[9] and both literacy and health programs on outside training. However, the health and literacy programs utilized Manobo supervisors who periodically visited the health workers and literacy teachers. AMBCI had a board of directors, not only in charge of the churches and pastors, but also given oversight of the literacy and health programs. Thus, AMBCI and its ministries resulted in a hierarchical network of linked leaders throughout much of Manobo territory. Further, the church was not in competition with the traditional leaders, but was generally respected by and worked in cooperation with the *datù*. The network of civil associations was thus in touch with the Manobo's political leaders, a fact that would prove important in succeeding years.

Finally, while the majority of Manobo adults learned to read through the vernacular literacy program, government-operated schools also played a part. As settlers intruded into new areas, the government established

---

[9] Funding has come from the Canadian International Development Agency and the Swedish International Development Cooperation Agency.

elementary schools within a few years. Some of the Manobo in those areas attended school. As a result, they not only learned to read, but also gained the cultural knowledge that would enable them to interact more effectively with mainstream Philippine society.

The role of religion

In attempting to understand the growth of the AMBCI, several factors are worth noting. First, the Philippine government has looked favorably upon the major variants of Christianity, including Roman Catholicism and most Protestant denominations. While I have never observed the government pressing the Manobo to adopt any form of Christianity (or any other religion), several Manobo have expressed that government officials accord them more respect now that the Manobo are identified as Christian. It is doubtful that this perception was a major motivation for adopting Christianity—the government's approval would provide little benefit in everyday life—but the government's favorable attitude may have reinforced religious choices made for other reasons.

Secondly, while the government and Philippine society in general endorses Christianity, the growth of the Manobo church seems best understood as religious resistance: adoption of a worldview that acknowledged their worth and that gave them conceptual tools to respond to the pressures they were being subjected to. This was not subjugation, as the Manobo did not take on their conquerors' religion; the Manobo adopted a generic Protestant Christianity, rather than the Roman Catholicism prevalent among the settlers. A major factor in this development was likely the availability of the New Testament in the Manobo language, and the absence of any external institution that wished to maintain control over the emerging church.[10] Had either Roman Catholic or Protestant denominational missionaries chosen to use the vernacular and to endorse Manobo leadership and control of congregations, the religious history of the Manobo may have turned out differently.

As it was, the AMBCI spread through a large portion of Manobo territory. As it did so, the church association not only preached, but also taught literacy, provided health care, and addressed the everyday concerns of the Manobo people. In the process, the church movement gave rise to a number of leaders active in various domains and in frequent communication with one another. Thus the church movement had an impact far beyond the religious domain, as it produced the network of civil associations that would eventually give rise to coordinated political resistance—the subject of the next chapter.

---

[10] SIL personnel, while motivated by a personal Christian commitment, do not accept positions of authority in any ecclesiastical structure. The leadership of the Manobo churches was thus entirely indigenous.

5

Germination: Resistance Begins 1989–1995

In the previous chapters, we have traced the transformations in the Manobo's social, economic, and political organization brought about by the intrusions of settlers and loggers, and have examined the emergence of civil associations that would become the foundation for the Manobo's coordinated political efforts to obtain rights to their ancestral lands. We will now go on to examine the emergence of religious resistance in chapter 7, the subsequent transition to economic resistance in chapter 8, and the culmination in political resistance in chapter 9.

The emergence of political resistance among the Cotabato Manobo has been a gradual process, and one not fully anticipated by any of the parties involved, including the members of SIL. The Erringtons, Johnstons, and Kerrs had focused on linguistic analysis of the Manobo language, translation, and vernacular literacy. Translators Association of the Philippines (TAP) members Nida Guil-an Apang and Mila Cagape later guided the expansion of the literacy program, while TAP nurses Melita Bawaan and Pacita Lábaro, along with SIL member Gret Kaiser Jordan, trained a number of Manobo as health care providers. Working together, they provided the training for the Manobo to institute a community-based vernacular literacy program and health care; translation of the New Testament into the Manobo language led to the establishment of Christian congregations and a church association.

While these activities—religion, literacy, and health care—are often promoted by their providers and accepted by the recipients as good in and of themselves, the organizations that deliver and manage them can turn into loci of resistance, in that the people empowered through them come to understand themselves as agents and not simply as objects. However, the progress of both empowerment and resistance may have greatly exceeded anything that SIL or TAP anticipated. This should not be surprising. Organizations take on their own lives, particularly when they come under the increasing autonomous control of local actors, as has clearly been the case of Manobo Christianity.

As noted in the last chapter, the Manobo churches had formed an association, the AMBCI, in response to the expectations of Philippine society and government. However, the AMBCI board was not concerned with only "spiritual" matters: local Manobo leaders asked the Erringtons if SIL could provide someone to assist them in economic development. In response, the Erringtons invited my wife and me to join the project. We did so in 1989, with the understanding that we would be serving the Manobo in whatever areas of development they considered important. The Manobo's first interests were to raise fish[1] in freshwater ponds and to grow irrigated rice; later interests were home gardens and conservation measures. We developed production methods appropriate to the Manobo's economic assets and infrastructure limitations and, working with language assistants, wrote manuals on those methods in the Manobo language. At my request, the AMBCI board of directors selected several men whom I trained as agricultural extensionists, who then taught these methods in their home areas. My focus at this point, though, is not on the training, or on the effectiveness or ineffectiveness of the extension program. What is significant here is that the Manobo, through the church association, had organized to deliberately and cooperatively seek to advance their economic condition. Essentially, a religious organization had spawned economic resistance.[2] This outcome may be surprising to observers who regard the secular and religious as separate domains, but was consistent with the Manobo's traditional understanding of religion.

However, the Manobo's concerns were not just economic. The people with whom I spoke on a daily basis, and the church association leaders, were also deeply concerned about secure access to land and personal security.

---

[1] These were tilapia (*Oreochromis niloticus*).

[2] Some may object that "resistance" is too strong a term to apply to matters of mere livelihood. It is noteworthy, though, that societies actively respond to pressures upon them in many different domains. By labeling such response "resistance" only when it occurs in the political realm, we overlook the fact that groups may learn to resist in one area and then go on to resist in the area of politics. It therefore seems more accurate to label all active response as "resistance," especially in cases where resistance in one domain leads to resistance in the political realm.

The events of those years, related by a number of informants,[3] show they had good cause:

> 1989—A detachment of logging company guards was stationed near a high, short bridge over the Kedakelan River, between Ludù and Kenalan. A Manobo man went to the detachment to ask a company employee for some tobacco, but failed to return to his home. One to two days later, two other Manobo went to find out what had happened to their companion; they also failed to return home. Things continued like this until eight Manobo had gone to the detachment; all had been detained by the guards. The eight were then led out to the bridge mentioned. One by one, each one was shot on the bridge and allowed to fall into the river. Settlers later told the Manobo what had happened.

> Late 1980s or early 1990s—M&S Co. guards were conducting an "operation" in Tagbaken, near Tubak. Around 5 a.m., the guards opened fire on a group of Manobo clustered around a fire. One woman fell into the fire and could not get out, and was burned and died. Others of the group were also killed or wounded.

> 1991—Two Manobo men, Lagbed Capitan and Lepeng Sabil, were on a trail from Dapulan to Mepayag to get their rice, which they had harvested, during a time that some M&S guards were conducting an "operation." The two men were never seen again. Shortly thereafter, company guards boasted to the Manobo that they had killed two big pigs. The Manobo discovered blood on rocks below a deep pool in the Kulaman River, near where the men were last seen. The guards' boast, coupled with the blood discovered near the Kulaman River, had convinced the Manobo that the guards seized and shot the men and then threw their bodies into the Kulaman River.

> 1991—During another "operation" by M&S guards near Tinapawan, Uweg "Fernando" Palisan, with his wives and children, and Amay Atit were traveling by foot when they realized that guards were coming. They hid, but the guards discovered and shot and killed Amay Atit.

> 1992—The M&S Co. sought to expel the Manobo from the village of Pokò Wayeg because the Manobo were farming in an area the company was claiming under an Industrial Forest Management Agreement (IFMA). The guards threatened that if the people did not leave the village in fifteen days that they would return and shoot them. Some village leaders requested help from the mayor of Lebak, who wrote a letter to the vice governor, who in turn wrote a letter to the company guard chief, telling him not to expel the Manobo. When

---

[3] The land rights history related in this chapter is drawn from interviews and meetings of land rights leaders, *datù*, and Manobo and Tiruray church association leaders and pastors, mostly from June 2005 through October 2006, supplemented by notes from observations and conversations from earlier years.

the Manobo leaders delivered the letter to M&S Company's chief guard he expressed considerable anger toward the two leaders, but did not attempt to expel the Manobo from Pokò Wayeg.

1992—The Manobo in the Elem area sought to have the government open an elementary school there. The local office for the Department of Environment and Natural Resources (DENR) recommended asking M&S to release the entire village site from its logging concession so that DENR could convert it to an Integrated Social Forestry (that is, community forestry) area. The residents of Elem petitioned M&S Co. accordingly, with the document signed by the heads of households in the village and five Manobo having official government titles. One resident donated land for the school. After several months of negotiations with various government offices, the Department of Education, Culture, and Sports (DECS) opened the school in time for the 1992–93 school year. However, M&S Co. never released the area of Elem from its concession.

1992—The Manobo leaders in the Elem area wrote to Victor Consuji, owner of M&S Co., requesting to meet with him to discuss ways to minimize conflict with the company due to its establishment of an "Industrial Tree Plantation" on Manobo farmland. The letter was accompanied by a census of those with farms in the area where the company intended to establish the plantation, an area which included seven villages: Elem, Selaban Telan, Tumbaga, Migtuduk, Pokò, Kiyumu, and Apaen.

1992—DENR issued Industrial Forest Plantation Management Agreement No. 020 to M&S Co. The agreement leased 11,835 ha of public forest land to M&S Co. for 25 years, with the possibility of renewal for another 25 years, to provide timber and non-timber products for domestic industries and export. As part of the agreement, the company was to plant 30 percent of the area within two years and 100 percent within five years, and to protect the area from forest fires. No rent would be collected during the first five years, one-half peso per hectare per year for the next five years, and one peso per hectare per year thereafter. (One peso is equivalent to two US cents.) With the daily wage being P70[4]—when the Manobo can find paying employment—the most the company will pay to rent a hectare of land one year is only one seventieth of a Manobo's daily wage.

1992—Without either informing the residents or asking their permission, M&S Co. began planting the farmland around the village of Elem to timber species.[5]

---

[4] If one weeds another's field now, he will earn P50–60 per day, and be fed twice. Alternatively, if he is paid in rice, he will receive 1 *supà* of rice, which is worth P70. If he does not wish to be fed, he will receive P70 cash. (Information from Elem residents Ador Apang, Lisitu Kalabaw, and Boy Timuway, September 2006.)

[5] bagras (*Eucalyptus deglupta* Blume), gmelina (*Gmelina arborea*), and mangium (*Acacia mangium*)

A step forward in that regard came in 1992, which also saw some growth in local government recognition of the Manobo. The AMBCI submitted a petition to the government requesting several improvements for the village of Danu (a water project, church building, school building, and medicine and rice), signed by Danu leaders. Although the request was not granted, the petition itself constituted a watershed in Manobo relations with the outside world. The submission of the letter marked a new confidence on the Manobo's part that they could approach the government. While the AMBCI began as a religious organization, it had developed in a manner consistent with the Manobo's traditional pragmatic this-worldly orientation toward the functions of religion. Having begun with primarily "religious" concerns, it had progressed to the organization of local economic development projects, and then taken a further step into institutional assertiveness and approaching the government itself. There was a functional expansion from religion, to micro-economics, to politics. As each new function was embraced, the earlier functions continued unabated.

More significantly, Lebak Mayor Sergio Sabio invited the Manobo to select a Manobo municipal councilman, and the leaders of 24 villages sent a letter in reply selecting Ulin Capitan as their choice. Later that year, the residents of several Manobo villages in Lebak petitioned the municipal council to ask that their villages be designated as a new, predominantly Manobo *barangay*, to be named Native Land. While that *barangay* has never materialized, the petition was one more step in a growing dialogue between the Manobo and the Philippine government. The Manobo were still politically weak, but they were becoming more assertive and receiving a growing hearing.

Even so, while there were some advances, they were far outweighed by the growing personal dangers and land insecurity due to the behavior of the logging company. In May 1993, the church association board of directors made contact with a Philippine non-governmental organization (NGO[6]) named the Philippine Agency for Intercultural Development (PAFID) that has assisted a number of Philippine indigenous peoples to secure rights to their ancestral lands.[7] (Significantly, the AMBCI's letter to PAFID was signed by not only the board of directors, but also by Manobo leaders holding positions in local government.) PAFID helps indigenous peoples in understanding and navigating the complex and protracted process of obtaining land rights. Some of their personnel visited the Manobo area in 1993 to assist the Manobo and Tiruray in drawing up the documents and maps needed

---

[6] Scholars and activists in the Philippines distinguish between governmental organizations (GOs), non-governmental organizations (NGOs), and people's organizations (POs). A people's organization is comprised of those residing within the community, while a non-governmental organization is comprised of outsiders. NGOs may be further distinguished by whether they operate internationally (international NGOs, or INGOs) or only within the country in question (national NGOs, or NNGOs).

[7] For further information on PAFID, see their website http://pafid.blogspot.com.

to apply to DENR for a Certificate of Ancestral Domain Claim (CADC), a document that gives a group collective rights to the use of an area for 25 years and that may be renewed.[8] The CADC has yet to be approved, but the Manobo had other successes. One of the AMBCI board wrote DENR's national director concerning M&S Co., with the result that the company temporarily stopped logging and planting trees on the Manobo's farmland. In Kalamansig, representatives from several Manobo villages, accompanied by PAFID personnel, asked the mayor to halt the company's efforts to plant their village areas to gmelina trees, and the Manobo prevailed. However, the incursions continued. In 1993, DENR surveyed the land around Elem, without consulting the Manobo. When residents asked for an explanation, the agency replied that they were surveying for a road. The Manobo questioned the reliability of that answer though, for soon afterward M&S Co. conducted its own survey and began planting the farmland around Elem to eucalyptus trees. When one of the Manobo leaders wrote to the company to request them to suspend planting, the manager replied that DENR had approved the planting and the company would not stop. The company also persisted in abuses against the Manobo, cutting down Manobo's banana and coffee groves and burning Manobo's houses in three villages.

The next major institutional watershed came when Manobo petitions finally began bearing fruit, as the outside world began to listen. In 1994, a "Fact Finding Team" comprised of representatives from several government offices, NGOs, and some Manobo leaders visited the Manobo area to investigate reports the Manobo had filed of abuse by the logging company. Manobo attending the hearings noticed that company employees were recording the names of those who were most vocal in denouncing the company; soon afterward, the company security force was reportedly hunting for some of the AMBCI and literacy program leaders, who went into hiding to protect their lives. The company also reportedly threatened PAFID personnel. DENR's head issued a temporary order suspending M&S Co.'s logging and planting. The company stopped planting timber species and threw out their timber seedlings, but began planting coffee and mango instead. At the same time, the company's abuses continued. Informants relate that in one village, the company's security chief accused a Manobo man of burning a field, and in response ordered the man's house burned down and struck the man in the face with his rifle butt, breaking some of his teeth.

In May 1995, the AMBCI applied for a CADC on behalf of all the Manobo. It was at this point that another major shift occurred: DENR and PAFID directed the Manobo to form five secular organizations, one for each municipality, to pursue their land rights. DENR and PAFID argued that this would protect the church association from becoming a target of those objecting

---

[8] The CADC arrangement is essentially identical to what is identified in the United States as a reservation, except that its continued existence is not guaranteed. Whether that difference becomes important in practice remains to be seen.

to changes in land tenure, and that the formation of a separate land rights association for each municipality would keep problems in one municipality from delaying the government's approval of the Manobo's land rights for the entire area.

At this point, then, pursuit of land rights passed from the AMBCI to other Manobo associations. Yet before continuing with the account, several points should be noted. It was the church association, rather than an explicitly political organization, that first sought land rights on behalf of the Manobo people. Part of the explanation for this is that the Manobo consider religion to deal with the here-and-now as well as the otherworld or afterlife. Also significant, though, is that the "social capital" established in civil associations was giving rise to political action. The literacy, health care, and church networks associated with the AMBCI had developed a higher degree of coordination and centralization: the literacy and health programs now had supervisors, and the churches were united under the AMBCI. Furthermore, the AMBCI had accepted oversight of the literacy and health programs and had launched an agricultural extension program. The Manobo's scattered villages had become increasingly linked through the growing network of civil associations, made possible in large measure by widespread adoption of a version of Christianity that eschewed violence. Amicable relations between the religious and secular leaders reinforced the emerging network of relationships. The AMBCI board had included Manobo government officials in their land rights efforts and were working in cooperation with them. And, when told that land rights would have to be pursued through secular associations, the AMBCI readily turned over that task. An effective foundation had been laid for the emergence of political resistance.

6

Seedlings: The Growth (and Death) of Local Organizations

We have been tracing the arc of a big story: of how the Manobo were invaded by outside forces that overturned their society, and how they have subsequently resisted, integrating into the dominant society by developing new forms of social organization that have enabled them to work toward common goals. As we have done so, we have seen demonstrated one of the central tenets of anthropology: that the various domains of culture are connected to one another, and that changes in one area often lead to changes in others. In the last chapter, we traced the emergence of political resistance from the foundations laid in civil associations. In the next, we will go on to examine the culmination of this process. But in order to understand the mechanisms by which the Manobo are mobilizing resistance—and which are at work among other indigenous peoples in similar circumstances—we will pause to examine the Manobo's civil organizations and take note of the factors that facilitated or obstructed their function. We will begin with the Manobo church association.[1]

Association of Manobo Bible Churches

Prior to the arrival of settlers (as defined in the preface) and the logging company, gatherings among the Manobo were limited in their complexity.

---

[1] The information on the Manobo church association is taken from interviews of the board of directors and selected members during January and September, 2006.

On those few occasions when one *datù* called other *datù* to join him to help decide a particularly difficult case, he provided the food needed from his own personal hospitality. When larger numbers of people came together for weddings and funerals, the food needed was provided and cooked by close kin. There were also occasional raiding parties, but the participants came from a small geographical area and the parties were disbanded once the raid was over. In contrast, the Manobo church association contains 114 congregations scattered over four municipalities. Dealing with the affairs of such a large and wide-spread organization has required the Manobo to develop social mechanisms absent from their traditional individualist social organization.

The Association's pastor training sessions are a primary factor driving the need for new social mechanisms. Twice each year, the pastors gather together for a seminar of three to five days, taught by the board members and other senior pastors. These seminars play a significant role in the development of networks among the Manobo, as they are the primary means for communication between the widely-separated board members, pastors, and congregations. Beyond this, though, the seminars have necessitated significant coordination. The teachers consult with each other to plan for the next seminar's topics and assign who will teach what. Providing meals for those attending requires the board to arrange for cooks, collect fees from the pastors, buy the food, and manage the supplies once they have been bought. The seminars also provide an occasion for board meetings and general meetings of the pastors. Thus, the seminars have resulted in a distinct increase in coordination over traditional culture. However, the transition has not been entirely smooth. The teaching usually is planned ahead of time. However, pastors frequently arrive several hours or a day after the seminar has begun, and seminar teachers sometimes arrive late as well. Provisions are especially problematic. The seminar fee, set by the pastors' general meeting, has been P100 for several years, but the average contribution is about P30. Contributions vary widely, with a few pastors giving the entire fee and several giving nothing. The treasurer usually does not arrive till shortly before the seminar starts, so those buying supplies cannot prepare beforehand. Lack of supplies has on several occasions led the board to end the seminar a day early. The board and pastors have discussed the problems with seminar funding several times, but no remedy has been reached, other than to reiterate that everyone needs to pay.

The AMBCI has taken several approaches to finances over the years. In 1990, soon after the association was registered, the pastors in a general meeting decided that each church would contribute annual dues of P1 per member, and would also give P100 toward a dedication ceremony for the new office building. A number of congregations gave what the pastors had committed to. However, after questions arose over management of the funds for the office building, contributions steadily decreased. The association also began having problems with transporting contributions to the treasurer. Transportation in the area is very expensive, so congregations found it impractical to carry their contributions directly to the treasurer. Instead, they would give them to a board member or senior pastor who happened to be passing through and ask that person to convey the funds to the treasurer. That sometimes took weeks or months, and the funds often ended up being used for some Association expenses by a local board member before reaching the treasurer. Consequently, the Association often had little in the way of funds, decisions were being made without the approval of the assembled board of directors, and some Association members were suspicious about how funds were being handled. In 1999, the pastors agreed that each church would contribute annual dues of P1 per member plus P100 per church, and appointed a fee collector for each municipality who would give the fees to the Association treasurer at the next seminar. Success was only partial: about one-third of the churches gave the per-member or per-congregation contribution, or both. One factor that may have contributed to arousing members' doubts regarding the AMBCI's funds is a lack of transparency. Some boards (elections are usually held every two years) failed altogether to make financial reports to the general meetings. The pastors debated the matter again in another meeting in 2005; suggestions included having each congregation give 10 percent of its income to the Association, having each member give P5, having each church give P500, and re-instating the original rule of every member giving P1 and every congregation giving P100. The pastors finally decided to return to the original rule. The congregations seem to have had some success in meeting their commitment; half a year later, about half of them had made the per-member or per-church contribution, or both.

As mentioned earlier, communication in the Manobo area is difficult. The seminars provide far more opportunity for face-to-face discussion than did the small and occasional gatherings of the traditional culture, but the board members and pastors have found this level of communication to be inadequate. However, there are substantial obstacles to improvement. Villages are far apart and travel by foot is time-consuming. Public motorized transportation is available on the few roads through Manobo territory, but is very expensive in terms of the Manobo's income; a round-trip to even nearby villages can easily cost a day's income. There are no telephone lines in the area. Cell phones have started to appear but are expensive, and the hilly terrain makes it difficult to obtain a connection. To deal with the communication problem, the AMBCI board decided they would like to purchase three motorcycles with which the board members could visit member churches. The motorcycles would be owned by the Association and operated as taxis whenever not used by the board members, thus generating income for the Association. Funds for the motorcycles' purchase would come from some foundation. No donor has been found, so the plan has never been put into practice. What is significant, however, is the concept of obtaining resources to meet the group's needs not from member churches but from some other source (in this case, from taxi fares and an outside donation). The Association has had other such plans. As early as 1991, some of the pastors, literacy teachers, health workers, and extension agents made contributions to start a cooperative store in Elem, though the store was never opened. In the fall of 2005, the pastors decided in a general meeting that they would establish cooperative projects in each of the villages where they usually have seminars. Income from the projects would then pay for their food when seminars came around. Each pastor was to contribute P500 at the fall 2006 seminar, when they would build a fishpond in the village where they would meet. However, the seminar came and went in October 2006 with only one pastor making a contribution.

Generalizing from these accounts, the Association has tried three approaches to obtaining operating funds: relying on contributions from its member churches, soliciting funds from outside agencies, and setting up income-generating projects. So far, the last two approaches have been unsuccessful, while the Association has had variable success with the first. The Manobo church association has ended up managing not only group funds, but also tangible group property. The literacy and health programs had, in various ways, acquired a few carabao and horses during the 1980s and 1990s. The literacy teachers and health workers decided that there would be fewer questions about the animals if they were placed under the AMBCI's jurisdiction. In 1999, the board debated what to do with the animals. They decided to keep the animals and use them on a group-owned farm, even though this would mean having to manage corporate property. While this is a significant departure from Individualist social organization, the board maintains only an incomplete knowledge of how the farm is progressing and of the disposition of income from it. In this matter, the AMBCI has not yet fully transitioned to managing the animals as group property.

The Manobo church association has demonstrated a sustained interest in obtaining the advantages of corporate organization. It has maintained itself without outside financing or control. But, it has also experienced significant problems in its financial affairs. Part of this can be attributed to the expense of transportation and lack of telephone service. However, the lack of transparency, the limited financial contributions from member churches, and the continued interest in seeking income from outside the membership are better explained by observing that the Association's leaders and members have only a limited commitment to group (that is, to group-ness). In short, the emergence of a new level of far-flung intercommunity coordination has automatically engendered the need for mechanisms of fund raising and fund management, a transition that will be familiar to students of NGO development in other settings as well.

Other civil associations

A number of other civil associations developed alongside the AMBCI. Some, such as the literacy program and network of clinics, had an official relationship. Others had no official relationship but, in a society that did not draw a sharp distinction between sacred and secular, were frequently initiated by both religious and secular leaders. We will examine several of these groups, beginning with some in which SIL or TAP played a significant role, and going on to other associations in which there was minimal or no outside involvement.

Agricultural extension

After my wife and I joined SIL's Manobo team in 1989, the first thing the Manobo approached us for was help in learning how to produce tilapia in freshwater fishponds. Using several sources on aquaculture, I designed a production system that relied on few external inputs, wrote a training manual, and with the help of two Manobo men, Ador Apang and Amay Luni Belag, translated it into the Manobo language. The Municipal Agriculture Office in Lebak provided us with fingerlings on two occasions, in mid-1990 and again in mid-1991. In each case, those who had built fishponds gathered in Elem for the fingerlings to arrive and then quickly transported them to their ponds. The approach at this point was highly informal. At my request, the ABMCI board chose nine men to be trained as agricultural extension agents; their first seminar was in May 1991. In contrast to the literacy and health programs, which had relied on funding from external sources and had supervisors who were to visit the practitioners, the extension program was designed to be consistent with Individualist social organization (cf. pp. 6–9). The livelihood teachers occasionally taught their neighbors how to build and manage fishponds, but there were no organized classes, no payment of teachers,[2] and no active management of the extension effort. Even so, fishponds began to spread, as shown by table 6.1.

---

[2] The training manual explained that the livelihood teachers were not paid and were not asking for payment, but also suggested that if trainees benefited from the teachers' training that they share a portion of the benefit they reaped. The livelihood teachers reported that they did receive some thank-you gifts, such as occasional portions of a fishpond harvest.

Table 6.1. Villages and persons having active fishponds

Date	Persons	Villages
August 1990	1	1
August 1991	5	2
November 1991	8	2
November 1991	11	3
April 1992	13	3
April 1992	14	4
April 1992	20	5
July 1994	32	6
September 1994	37	6
July 1995	40	7
1997	39	15
2006	63	20

The next farming technique the Manobo were interested in was irrigated rice production. The Manobo have grown rice for generations—no one can remember hearing of a time they had not—but have grown the crop as upland rice, depending on natural rainfall. They knew that most Filipinos grow rice using irrigation and wanted to adopt the technique, so asked if we could help them to learn how. As with the fishponds, I consulted several published sources on rice production, devised a system that minimized external inputs, wrote a training manual and, with the help of Ador Apang and Anduy Nayam, translated the manual into Manobo. The manual was published in 1993 and made available through the literacy program. The livelihood teachers began using it to teach their neighbors how to build and manage rice paddies, while some farmers read and followed the manual on their own. As with the fishponds, there was no organized effort to teach irrigated rice production, but the technique spread (table 6.2 and table 6.3).

Table 6.2. Villages practicing promoted enterprises

| | Number of villages having promoted enterprise | | | | | | | |
| | Fishponds | | Basakan | | Gardens | | Any | |
Region	1997	2006	1997	2006	1997	2006	1997	2006
Danu/Pokò	5	9	4	1	2	15	7	16
Linàlaan	2	3	0	3	0	8	3	8
Ludù	5	1	3	1	6	7	6	7
Migàgà	3	7	1	4	1	5	3	7
Total	15	20	8	9	9	35	19	38

Table 6.3. Persons practicing promoted enterprises

| | Number of persons having promoted enterprise | | | | | | | |
| | Fishponds | | Basakan | | Gardens | | Total | |
Region	1997	2006	1997	2006	1997	2006	1997	2006
Danu/Pokò	11	35	6	1	10	190	27	226
Migàgà	12	27	1	12	1	45	14	84
Ludù	14	1	14	3	129	69	157	73
Linàlaan	2	0	0	0	0	10	2	10
Total	39	63	21	16	140	314	200	393

The extension program had been designed to be consistent with an Individualist social organization, in which individuals may cooperate for brief periods of time for defined purposes but establish no on-going structures. Teachers were not expected to establish or adhere to a fixed schedule of classes (individual farmers arranged training with a particular extension agent for whenever it was convenient for both parties), and there were no supervisors who had to regularly visit the teachers. Consistent with the non-hierarchical nature of Individualist societies, relationships were peer-to-peer; there was no expectation of accountability to supervisor. Avoidance of funding made this even easier, as there were no funds that had to be accounted for, either to funding agencies or to the teachers' neighbors. Avoidance of funding also fit a still heavily cash-free economy. The livelihood teachers were not paid, but were instead recompensed on an informal, in-kind basis, very much as the maker of a basket was not paid by the recipient, but could eventually expect some kindness in return.[3]

[3] The teachers also received informal compensation in the form of increased status (that is, standing within the group, traditionally called "rank" in anthropology); I often heard them referred to by other residents of their villages as *Mistelu* 'Teacher'.

Tables 6.1–6.3 suggest the result of accommodating the extension program to the Manobo's culture. There is no "control," where the exact same techniques were promoted to communities of essentially identical culture by different approaches (for example, promoting communal fishponds with mandatory labor by all in the village, or the establishment of a hierarchical and heavily structured extension network), so statistical analysis of the results is not possible. Even so, the survey data demonstrate that fishponds and irrigated rice culture attained noteworthy adoption without the establishment of a typical extension program, suggesting that accommodation of the program to Manobo culture was an effective approach, and that consideration of a group's social organization could make development efforts more effective in other cultures as well.

Elem clinic

As noted before, SIL and TAP had established literacy and health programs among the Manobo. When we joined SIL's work with the Manobo, our SIL and TAP colleagues expected my wife and me to help those programs become fully community-based, meaning that they would be conducted, governed, and funded by the communities they served. Our experiences with the Elem-area health workers helped to reconfirm the Individualist nature of Manobo society and the value of fitting programs to the society's social organization. In 1991, the health workers in Elem, Bitogen, and Danu decided to establish a group agricultural project to generate income for their clinics. They chose to grow a field variety of maize in Danu, which is located along a road, and sell the grain. Travel between Danu and the other two villages at that time was usually by foot and took two to three hours. Thus, it was evident that not all the health workers could participate in growing the crop, but they decided to go ahead with the group venture, evidently deciding they could make more money through cooperation than through individual effort. The funds to start the project were provided by a church in the United States.

The leadership of the project appears to have been diffuse, shared between a health worker living in Danu and a health worker supervisor living in Elem. Danu-area health workers contributed labor, but the project also paid non-health workers for a variety of services, such as plowing. In the end, the project made a "negative profit," losing 17 percent of its starting capital. The immediate causes of the losses were high expenses for seed, labor, and food for participating health workers, as well as having to pay a portion of the crop to the land-owner. However, the more fundamental problem was loose management. It appeared that far less oversight was given to the group project than was typical for privately owned crops. The following year, the health workers decided that coffee would be more profitable than field maize. They used the remaining capital to obtain a coffee grove in Danu and did make some harvests from it. However, almost all of the income was borrowed by various members of the group. The project was dissolved at the end of 1995 with partial repayment of the loans, minimal profit, and confused bookkeeping. As with the earlier maize crop, group ownership of the project had failed to produce income for the clinics, and had even failed to benefit all the participants individually. It was evident that the health workers expected some benefit from cooperating with each other, but the corporate group-ownership approach had failed.

This observation led my wife and me to consider the workings of the clinics themselves. When TAP nurses Pacita Lábaro, Melita Bawaan, and Diolia Galorport trained the health workers and helped them establish clinics, the explicit understanding with the villages' leaders and residents was that the clinics were village enterprises, owned and under the control of the village, though staffed by the health workers (who were also village residents). The clinics were thus corporate affairs. Unfortunately, they usually had little medicine on hand and were owed large amounts by patients who had been treated but never paid for their medicine. The clinic in Elem serves as an example. The building had been constructed by Registered Nurse Gret Kaiser Jordan, an SIL member who lived in Elem from 1987 through 1989 and trained six health workers during that time. After her departure, the clinic was staffed by the health workers she had trained. The medicine they used was originally provided by Jordan, but patients were to pay for both the medicine and treatment so that the medical supplies could be replenished. By the time my wife and I arrived in 1989, the clinic seldom had medicine on hand. We talked with people in the village about the situation, but continued to have difficulty understanding the situation until we studied the Manobo's general social organization in 1991, followed by examination of their agricultural system in 1994. The results of those studies (Fraiser and Fraiser 1991) showed Manobo usually acted as Individualists. We discussed this perception with the Manobo health workers and later with the entire community. In October 1994, the health workers and community decided to "privatize" the clinic. Instead of a single village-owned clinic, there would now be six individual clinics, each owned by the health workers running it. Pricing of medicine would continue to be subject to village control, to prevent any health worker from asking an exorbitant amount. However, each health worker would maintain his (or her) own stock of medicine and would manage his own funds. In January 1995 (residents are still receiving income from coffee sales during January, so they could pay their debts), each of the health workers collected the debts he had permitted or made up the difference from personal funds. Then the health workers purchased medicine and divided it equally among themselves. The clinic had essentially been transformed from a partnership with six equal members to six separate enterprises.

The results were mixed. By September 1995, none of the health workers had medicine on hand; all of it had been dispensed to patients on
credit. However, once coffee season (typically November through January)
arrived, some of the health workers were able to collect the debts owed
them, bought new medicine, and treated patients until the end of coffee
season, at which point they again dispensed medicine on credit and ceased
to function. Observation of small housefront stores in the village followed
the same pattern: the stores functioned and ran a profit during coffee season, sold their stock on credit at the end of the season, and then collected
the debts owed them and reopened the following coffee season. The clinics, like the privately run village stores, went dormant during the low-cash
months, but functioned again during coffee season. Accommodation to the
society's current social organization produced a health system that did not
fully meet either the Manobo's or TAP's or SIL's desires, but that was far
more effective than what had been produced using a corporate (that is,
organized group) approach.

While adapting the health care program to the Manobo's traditional
social organization has evidently been more effective, recent events suggest
that the Manobo continue to be interested in capturing the advantages of
greater coordination. While I was in Elem in June 2005, Sulutan Edod
Nayam suggested that the village return to having a single clinic. The
clinic had been privatized almost twelve years earlier and, though the
health workers occasionally had medicine—an improvement over the
performance of the village-owned clinic—village residents wanted better
health services. In a village meeting, the residents decided to rebuild the
clinic building and elected officers who would oversee its operation. Some
of the residents disassembled the old clinic, with the intent of using the
materials to construct a new and smaller building. However, it became
apparent that most of the materials had deteriorated too far to be reused.
As of November 2006, the new clinic was still unbuilt. The carpenters did
not have the wood and metal roofing needed, and no one among the health
workers or elected project leaders had spoken to the residents to ask for
contributions. It appears that the social costs of cooperation overshadowed
the immediate benefits.

Fruit trees

I described earlier the establishment of the agricultural extension program
and the results of designing programs in a manner that takes into account
the absence in Manobo society of traditions of sustained supra-household
coordination. The approach resulted in the spread of both tilapia production
and irrigated rice culture among the Manobo; however, the rate of adoption
varied from one region or technique to another between areas and techniques, despite these being methods in which the Manobo had expressed

an interest. Discussions with the extension agents revealed that overly hilly topography made fishponds and rice paddies impractical in many places. Another technique the Manobo had been interested in was SALT (sloping agricultural land technology), a system in which nitrogen-fixing hedges are planted on the contour in cropland at intervals designed to minimize soil erosion; the hedges in turn provide nitrogen and organic matter to the soil. However, while experiments had shown the system provided very good returns to both labor and capital elsewhere in the Philippines due to increased yields, the start-up costs were too high to make it practical for the cash-poor Manobo to adopt. It was evident that if the Manobo were to improve their standard of living, other techniques or enterprises would be needed. In 1995, I visited the villages where the livelihood teachers were active to ask the residents what activities they thought would be both promising and realistic. Each of the villages I visited expressed an interest in growing tree fruits. I was skeptical at first: tree fruits in the Philippines are highly profitable but also perishable, and roads were distant from most villages and not always open. However, the farmers were certain they could transport their produce to the road (and if need be to market) by animal or on their own backs. The livelihood teachers and I therefore proceeded to investigate how the Manobo could obtain the trees they wanted.

As in the case of promoting fishponds and irrigated rice culture, the fruit tree program was designed to fit an Individualist society: there would be no sustained structures of cooperation and no hierarchy, but there would be temporary cooperation among peers for a single purpose. We would buy the seedlings as a group in order to minimize transportation costs per tree and obtain a better price. However, each farmer would select what he wanted to plant, pay for his own trees, and plant them on his own property. The trees had to be planted at the beginning of the rainy season (the end of April) to ensure they would be well established before the dry season began, but money was scarce at that time, though available during coffee harvest (November-January). Hence, the livelihood teachers and I would visit the villages taking part in the program during January to collect farmers' payments and place them in a bank account in Kalamansig (several signatures would be required for withdrawal, to guard against embezzlement and suspicion), and then buy the trees in early April, right before planting.

The next task was to find a good source of fruit tree seedlings. I contacted the government agricultural offices in three municipalities (Kalamansig, Lebak, and Sen. Ninoy Aquino) to ask if they could sell fruit trees at a reduced cost. Kalamansig's Municipal Agriculture Officer (MAO; the same abbreviation is used for both the office and the officer) Orlando Tongcua suggested the farmers form a cooperative to interface with the MAO, but was very willing to obtain seedlings from a government nursery outside the province at a much lower cost than available locally. Tongcua told us the price for each kind of tree. The livelihood teachers collected the farmers' payments in January 1996 and deposited them in a bank in Kalamansig. The MAO in turn ordered the trees we were asking for and cared for them in their own nursery until April, when we paid for the trees. Kalamansig Mayor Meinardo Concha provided a dump truck to transport the trees to two separate villages, from which the participants carried them to their farms. The only external funding was P200 from SIL given to the Kalamansig government to help pay for fuel for the dump truck. Fifteen farmers from eight village municipalities bought 210 trees that year and planted them on their own land (table 6.4).

Table 6.4. Fruit tree planting

Year	Participation			Number of seedlings			Cost, Philippine pesos			
	Farmers	Villages	Municipalities	Fruit trees	Coconut	Total	Fruit trees	Coconut	Fuel charge	Total
1996	15	8	1	210		210	7,830	0	0	7,830
1997	184	18	2	1,079	420	1,499	43,475	6,300	1,089	49,124
1996–1997[a]	189	21	2	1,289	420	1,709	51,305	6,300	1,089	56,954

[a] Note: The two-year participation figures are not totals of the single-year figures, as some farmers, villages, and municipalities participated both years.

Several Manobo asked to repeat the project the next year. That time, the MAO in Sen. Ninoy Aquino was also able to obtain trees for the Manobo. (The MAO in Lebak had also planned to obtain fruit trees, but was unable to when the municipal budget was not approved.) As before, funds were collected in January and deposited in a bank (I helped the livelihood teachers in Sen. Ninoy Aquino municipality open a bank account there), purchases were made in April, the MAOs obtained the trees, and the mayors provided transportation. In 1997, 184 farmers in 18 villages, over two municipalities, bought 1,499 fruit trees. Each farmer paid for the trees he had selected and planted them on his own land.

Unexpected weather caused problems after the second planting. An El Niño occurred during 1998 and the resulting drought killed roughly one-half of the trees planted in 1997. I expected that the participants might be discouraged by the frustrations of their efforts, but the farmers I talked with were instead encouraged that some of the trees had survived. Even with the damage caused by the drought, many farmers had obtained fruit trees that they could expect to provide improved income in the future. Accommodating the program to the Manobo's Individualist social structure—pursuing short-term cooperation while avoiding the creation of an institution or procedure that would require on-going cooperation—had enabled the Manobo to obtain a goal that was beyond the practical scope of individual action.

Belanga literacy program

The projects in these three areas—promotion of fishponds and irrigated rice culture, provision of village-level health care, and obtaining fruit tree seedlings—were designed to fit Individualist social cooperation. Ownership and control were kept at the individual level, avoiding the creation of structures that would require on-going cooperation and hierarchy. This enabled the projects to achieve their goals, while simultaneously avoiding creating organizations unlikely to continue or to function without outside involvement. At the same time, the projects reinforced the social standing of the health workers and livelihood teachers and added to the civil relationships that could be utilized for purposes of political resistance.

TAP's literacy program in the Manobo village of Belanga evinced a greater level of cooperation.[4] When funding from the Canadian International Development Agency that the literacy program depended on to pay the teachers and supervisors became uncertain, the literacy teachers in Belanga instituted an in-kind registration fee for their students. Through this, the literacy teachers obtained ten bundles of green onions, which they used to start a literacy cooperative. They multiplied the onions over a few seasons, finally selling the crop for P4,000, which they used to buy a coffee grove of about 0.25 hectares. They made a share-cropping arrangement with a village resident, who weeds the grove and picks and dries the coffee, in return for which he receives one-half of the coffee he harvests. The literacy teachers have used the income to provide books for the literacy program. The trees have now gotten old and many have died from an invasive vining weed, but the grove produced significant funds for the program for several years. The literacy teachers plan to replace the trees and continue the cooperative.

Several factors appear to have contributed to the greater level of cooperation demonstrated in the Belanga literacy cooperative. First, a group of Manobo had established the village as essentially a religious colony (cf. pp. 73–74); this explicit ideological uniformity may have led to fewer tensions and greater cooperation. Furthermore, the original pastor-*datù* (Datù Pidal Utub) and his successor as pastor (Salab Utub) have both been well respected by the villagers and have led by working to build consensus. Finally, the members of TAP who lived there from 1982 through 1993, Pacita Lábaro and Mila Cagape, left direction of local activities to village leaders while mentoring them in the management of those activities.

---

[4] The information on the Belanga literacy program comes from a focus group of Belanga literacy teachers and supervisors, and an interview of Mila Cagape, TAP literacy specialist, both conducted in February, 2005.

Associations with minimal outside involvement

We now turn to consider another category of civil associations, namely, those that were solely or primarily under the control of the Manobo. While these groups were, like those of the livelihood program, also economically oriented, they were free from pressure to conform to my inclinations of what would be most successful, and thus more representative of the Manobo's preferences and assumptions.

"Health insurance": The Elem pig project

When my wife and I moved to Elem in 1989, the village had a clinic and several health workers.[5] However, money for medicine was readily available only during coffee harvest, from November through January. Several residents expressed a desire to get around this problem. My wife and I thought we might have a solution when a US church provided some "seed money" as start-up capital for a project to help fund the clinics. Notice it was already assumed that there should be a communally-owned and operated project. My wife and I, and the Elem residents I talked with, readily accepted this assumption. The residents I talked with decided that income for health care should be generated by raising pigs. They would purchase piglets using the seed money and, once the number of piglets had grown, they would return the seed money, which would then be used to start a project in another village. From that point on, all subsequent returns would go to the participants. Each person would have his own account at the clinic, to be used for medicine whenever a family member needed treatment. The effort would begin as a group project, with several people raising each piglet, because we had too little money to buy a piglet for each participant.

The project began in April 1991, with three groups of four persons each, and the twelve participants chose one of themselves as project coordinator. By November 1992, the number of pigs had increased enough to have just two persons per pig. Each person's clinic account was credited for one piglet, and we bought medicine equivalent to that amount, to be kept in the clinic. However, the project began having problems the next year. In January 1993, two persons borrowed piglets in a *sagud* arrangement; once the pig was grown and slaughtered, one-half the gross profit would go to the clinic and one-half to the one who raised the pig. Essentially, they were using the clinic project to produce personal income, rather than to guarantee they would have medicine when needed. By July 1993, the arrangement had taken over as the project's governing principle. It became apparent at the same time that the common Philippine practice of selling on credit was causing problems for the project. With the debt owed to an

---

[5] The information for this section comes from my notes on the pig project during its operation.

abstract corporate entity rather than a concrete individual, the debts were not readily collected. Additionally, not all of the money collected for sales was being passed on to the treasurer.

The financial problems and the conversion of the project from one bolstering health care to simply providing another source of income might have been prevented had I, as an outsider, taken the role of manager. However, the more fundamental problem seems to be that we had set up a system that depended on sustained cooperation, including the exercise of hierarchy and a shared understanding of what constituted acceptable behavior.

Cooperative stores

The most common type of cooperative I have observed among the Manobo is a store, modeled on the ubiquitous *sari-sari* store seen throughout the Philippines.[6] *Sari-sari* is a Tagalog word meaning "a little of everything," and that is exactly what these small, house-front stores sell: small quantities of goods such as rice, sugar, cooking oil, and soy sauce, cans of sardines, little tubes of toothpaste, candy by the piece, etc. Most villages have at least one such store, and in towns these stores are frequently just a short walk away. In the Manobo's cooperative store ventures, the members each contribute start-up capital and then receive income in proportion to their contribution. In the case of the Manobo cooperative stores, the stores also usually functioned as a coffee middleman, buying coffee berries and beans and selling them in the *barangay* or municipal seat for a profit.

Elem cooperative store #1

Elem's first cooperative store was conceived of by Amay Pidelu[7], who later became the village pastor. The store was started in 1982[8] by nine men, each of whom contributed P90 for start-up capital. They chose one of their number as treasurer; he and one other member were the store-keepers. There was no auditor (an officer in most Philippine cooperatives, whose job it is to periodically review the treasurer's records), but Amay Pidelu helped with the records, as he had had several years of formal schooling. Loans were forbidden unless agreed upon by the entire group. The cooperative began just after rice threshing and lasted to the same time the following year, when the

---

[6] Information on the cooperative stores, the Elem chainsaw cooperative, and the Belanga women's group come from focus groups comprised of the vast majority of members of each organization, supplemented by observations made and interviews conducted during the times of operation.

[7] This is a pseudonym.

[8] This is an approximate date, determined by the informants' references to other events.

treasurer gave an account to the members. They found out that the store had made some losses, but more importantly, that the treasurer had lent someone a portion of the money. The treasurer would not say to whom the money was lent, and has since died. The members decided not to continue with the store and dissolved it. Of the other eight members, four of them received back a portion of their initial investment, and four received nothing.

Elem cooperative store #2

The second cooperative store, like the first, was the idea of Amay Pidelu. It was begun in 1985 or 1986[9] by ten men, with a starting capital of about P1,200. The group chose two men who had received some formal education to clerk the store. The group chose one clerk to be treasurer and the other plus a literacy graduate to be auditors. The cooperative lasted almost two years. The former members commented that the management was good because they had gotten their initial investment back. However, despite running for two years, there was little profit distributed. One member got P20 and another P30. Other informants did not give figures but said they had received a small amount of money. Despite the fact that such low profit suggests either gross mismanagement or malfeasance, the members did not discuss the loss with the managers, because it would hurt the managers' feelings.

Elem cooperative store #3

The third store was, again, the idea of the village pastor. However, the members this time were women. Each of the thirty-two members contributed P100 start-up capital, for a total of P3,200. The pastor served as treasurer, while an unrelated man served as auditor. The pastor chose a single woman as store-keeper, as she would not have children who might eat merchandise without paying for it. She was to receive 20 percent of the profits as compensation for her services. The pastor also set forth the rules for how the store was to be run, including a prohibition against allowing anyone to buy on credit. Cooperative members were to be charged the same prices as non-members.

The store was intended to stay open year-round, rather than closing at the end of coffee season, as was common for small stores. However, it survived only a few months, from October 1995 to February 1996. It was supposed to figure its profit and pay a dividend to its investors at the end of each month, but the managers never reported its financial status until it collapsed. Most of the members received back their investment, plus a small portion of the leftover goods owned by the store; some lost even the capital they had invested. Some of the cooperative's money had been lost through selling goods on credit. However, the thing that informants credited with bringing

---

[9] This date is approximate, determined by the informants' references to other events.

down the store was that the treasurer (the village pastor) had mortgaged a horse belonging to him and a village leader to the store, and had then taken the horse back without returning the money. Additional money was "lost" by the store-keeper in buying and selling coffee.

The cooperative members appeared to be deliberately vague as to whether they thought the money had been lost or stolen or embezzled, so I inquired whether anyone had attempted to settle the matter. It turned out that no one had. The problem with the horse had come first, so those who might judge the case—the village leader and the pastor—were in no position to investigate the store-keeper's loss of money. After the cooperative disintegrated, the store-keeper moved to another village and opened a store there.

Elem cooperative store #4

The fourth store was the venture of eighteen men and one woman. Investments varied from P200 to P1,000 per person. The group chose one woman and one man, both of whom had their own families, to manage the store; they were to receive 20 percent of the profit as compensation. The cooperative began in October 2003 and was terminated the following February. As that is the month when those practicing swidden agriculture clear their fields in preparation for planting, one of the store-keepers needed to direct her attention to farming, and many of the members wanted their money to buy food for work parties to clear their fields. All the members received back their principal; most also received a portion of the profit, roughly proportional to their investment. Some received their profits in cash; others, in goods. Significantly, the village pastor was not involved in either the fourth or fifth store.

Elem cooperative store #5

The fifth store was a cooperative venture between three men, each of whom invested P500. It ran from October 2004 to February 2005. They chose a young divorcée who had completed part of high school as the store-keeper. As with the third store, she received 20 percent of the profit as compensation. The owners also told her they would give her food if she needed anything. Unlike the third store, this one did not buy and sell coffee, as the store-keeper did not have the strength to transport it to market. After four months, one member withdrew money from the store for his own business purposes. Another member became suspicious but did not want to make a confrontation, so suggested closing the store, and the others agreed. Each member received back his investment, plus some sardines and rice.

Mayul cooperative

The village of Mayul also has a cooperative. The village has 42 families and 264 residents, of whom about 100 are adults, making it a sizable village, though smaller than Elem. Two months after Florentino Kapitan, the current *sitio* leader, was elected into office, he had the idea of starting a community cooperative and discussed the idea with others in the village. Twenty-nine of them decided to become members. The group planted two crops of maize, from which they derived P5,500, at which point they met to consider what to do next. They decided to start a store and elected cooperative officials. Florentino was elected president; Tony Kapitan, treasurer; Villamor Kapitan, auditor; and Lito Bautista, secretary. The elected officials in turn appointed the store's staff. Two women were selected as store-keepers, and Florentino was appointed to take produce the store bought from residents (coffee, maize, and chickens) and sell it to merchants in the nearby town of Ketudak. The officials also set out rules for the store. Members could buy on credit but had to pay off their debts within four days. The store-keepers could not loan money to anyone unless all the officials first met together to approve the loan. When a store-keeper went to buy supplies for the store, he had to record how much money he took and how much he returned, and had to obtain the signature of the motorcycle driver who transported the supplies.

The store-keepers, cooperative officers, and cooperative members met together periodically to review the store's financial situation and make decisions. By the time of their first meeting in February 2003, the store had amassed P40,000. The members considered whether to place the money in a bank account or invest in a chainsaw. They chose to buy a chainsaw, selected an operator, and made rules regarding the saw: only the chosen operator could use it; payment would be made to the treasurer alone; he would in turn give the operator his proper share, and deposit the remainder with the store.

When they audited the cooperative a year later, the store and chainsaw had amassed over P72,000. The members debated whether to buy a water pump or a motorcycle and chose to buy a new motorcycle, putting down P30,000 and paying the remainder over two years. They then selected a driver and made rules for the motorcycle's use. The driver could not lend out the motorcycle to others, and both members and non-members had to pay for rides. Furthermore, the motorcycle had to return to Mayul every night, unless there was some great need, to ensure it remained based in Mayul. The driver could not operate the motorcycle on Sundays, unless it was to transport patients. Finally, the driver could not consume alcohol prior to operating the motorcycle.

The cooperative was audited again in May 2005, at which point it had almost P150,000. The group bought a cell phone and camera and designated that the remaining available funds be used for monthly payments on the motorcycle. By that time, the cooperative had also paid over half the cost of constructing a government-operated nutrition center in the village. (The government paid the remainder.) The store was left with working capital of about P10,000; outstanding debts, for goods sold on credit, were also about P10,000.

The cooperative ran up substantial expenses in mid-2005 when a cholera outbreak hit the village. The disease can kill quickly, and it was imperative that patients get to the municipal hospital without delay. However, coffee season was long past, and most residents did not have the cash on hand needed for transportation. The cooperative motorcycle ended up taking several patients to the hospital on credit. By early 2006, some of the families had paid their debts, but many had not. Even so, the cooperative was still solvent at the close of 2006.

Migàgà cooperative store

Another cooperative store operated in the village of Migàgà in the early part of this decade, at one point amassing P16,000. However, a measles epidemic struck the village in 2003, killing 20 people, and the cooperative distributed its funds to its members so they would have something to use in the emergency. The village has plans to reconstitute the cooperative but has yet to do so.

Summary

The prime motivation for the cooperative stores appears to have been capturing a profit, normally available only to outside merchants, through cooperation with other villagers. Members of the Mayul cooperative added that they wanted a cooperative store so they could have a place to buy food on credit when they lacked cash. Pressure from Mayul's *barangay* government also played a role in making a cooperative attractive there, as villages that could not make a contribution to the annual *barangay* fiesta were required to hold a "benefit dance"[10] and cock fight to raise the money. Mayul residents expressed that the dancing and gambling encouraged immoral behavior, and that they could keep them out of the village by having the cooperative make the required fiesta contribution on the village's behalf.

Of the seven cooperative stores studied, only the store in Mayul has continued to operate. Two were voluntarily brought to an end when participants had need for their assets: the fifth store in Elem was liquidated when the members needed their funds to prepare their fields for planting, while the store in Migàgà was dissolved when members needed funds to respond to a measles outbreak. The most common cause of dissolution

---

[10] In a benefit dance, anyone asking for a particular tune to be played makes a contribution to the dance organizers.

was members becoming concerned that their financial rights were being violated—that is, violation of trust. More significantly, such violation of trust invariably led to the store's demise. The Mayul cooperative stands in distinct contrast to most of those in Elem; it has operated for over four years, continually running a profit, and has kept the same officers throughout. Members' comments suggest that a significant factor in its survival is greater horizontal coordination—that is, the members have come to accept as normative that they have an obligation to the group, and have surrendered a portion of their independence to it. When I asked Mayul cooperative members what had enabled their cooperative to succeed while similar ventures had usually failed in Elem, one replied that they did not have a personal interest in the cooperative—that is, they did not regard the cooperative as part of their personal property, but as belonging to the group. Other members said that cooperatives elsewhere had failed because their members bought on credit and then did not pay, since they considered the cooperative's goods to be their own personal property. Mayul's pastor added that members must follow the cooperative's rules. He later shared that the village had had another cooperative store a few years earlier, but that it had failed due to a man who had since moved away. The cooperative had amassed several thousand pesos when the man lent a large part of the money to another village, which never repaid the loan. When members heard of it, they began buying from the store on credit and not repaying, eventually leading to the store's demise. The pastor concluded by saying that cooperatives cannot survive if they include people like that. Significantly, he made no mention of the possibility of barring such a person from becoming a member or gaining power, or of expelling or punishing the offender. Interestingly, one Elem resident had reported that Mayul fined those who violated village ordinances. When I asked the pastor about this, he replied that anyone who disrupted the village peace had to pay a fine of P5,000 (about 100 days' wages). However, no one had ever been fined, because no one had ever violated the rule. The pastor explained that rules were there in order to avoid having problems. It appears that while the village has not developed the capacity to impose sanctions, it has developed sufficient group cohesion to pressure residents to conform to group norms, without actually forcing them to do so. The community's smaller size, which would be expected to contribute to community cohesion, may be partially responsible. However, the personal integrity of community leaders stands out as particularly important, as the group appears to lack the capacity to punish behavior that undermines the cooperative.

Inability to punish negative behavior also stood out in the comments of former members of Elem's cooperative stores. One village leader was emphatic that he would never participate in another cooperative, while several others said they would, provided that the cooperative had rules so that those who err are punished. One man commented that the rules would not be enforced so long as the Manobo exercised *kesehiduway*—that is, extended mercy or forgiveness to one another. These days, he said, if someone sees someone stealing from him, he does nothing because of taking pity on the thief. Acceptance of the errors of close kin has been a feature of traditional Manobo culture, and appears to have been reinforced by the Manobo's emphasis of New Testament passages on forgiveness.

Elem chainsaw cooperative

There is another type of cooperative among the Manobo that I will call a chainsaw cooperative. In the highlands of Sultan Kudarat province (and probably in rural areas throughout the Philippines), sawyers fell trees and cut lumber by hand using chainsaws. Often, the saw is owned by a person having better finances and operated by someone else. The price paid for the lumber is divided following an agreed-upon proportion between the saw owner, the saw operator, and the person owning the tree from which the lumber is cut. Prior to 1995, a few settlers were cutting lumber in the Elem area. Several Manobo individuals and communities in the Elem area wanted lumber to build houses and churches, and decided to form a cooperative in order to obtain better prices than those offered by the settlers, and to capture some of the profit from lumber production for themselves. Each of the members was to receive access to lumber at a discounted rate, plus a portion of the profit commensurate with the capital he contributed. Twenty-four men and eight churches contributed the start-up capital. The amounts given by each party varied, with some giving as little as P50, while one church gave P10,500.

The group chose a treasurer, an operator, and an operator's helper. The operator was to cut lumber, take care of the chainsaw, and pass on all income received to the treasurer. The treasurer, in turn, would give the operator and his helper their proper shares, and also pay for the saw's operating expenses (gasoline, oil, and repairs). Non-members were to pay P5 per board-foot of lumber. Of that, the usual practice was for the owner to receive 90 percent; the operator, 8 percent; and the operator's helper, 2 percent. The owner paid for all operating expenses, while the operator and his helper paid for their own living expenses. However, the Elem chainsaw cooperative decided to modify this. Sixty percent of gross income was to go to the cooperative and 40 percent to the operator, who in turn would feed his helpers and pay them a wage of P50 per day (at that time a good wage in that region for an unskilled laborer). The cooperative would charge P5 per board-foot, which was similar to what private sawyers were charging. Members would be charged as though they were the saw's owner: they would pay P2 per board-foot (that is, the operator's 40 percent share of P5), and provide whatever gasoline and oil was needed (that is, cover operating expenses). Members could obtain however much wood they needed to build a house or church building, after which they were to pay the same rate as non-members.

The cooperative began cutting lumber in April 1995. By January 1996, the cooperative had cut P10,000 worth of lumber, all for members. However, much of the wood had been sold on credit. Additionally, some of the cash received had been lent out. One loan was to a coalition of four villages that was starting its own chainsaw cooperative, while the remainder was loaned to another village. The treasurer of the Elem cooperative had little cash on hand. Members began to complain about the cooperative's management. In September of that year, I asked a neighbor how many members were in the cooperative and received an unusually heated answer. One of his relatives was a member of the cooperative, but so far no one had received any income from it. My neighbor saw the chainsaw cooperative as being identical to the cooperative stores: whoever ran the cooperative used the money for his own purposes, while members did not benefit. Asked whether the problem might be that those running the cooperative did not know accounting, he replied that one store owner in the village could tell you how much profit he had made the previous year. To this informant, the problem was not lack of skill or knowledge.

The cooperative disintegrated sometime after this. Of five former members I spoke with, one had received back most of his investment, but the others had lost theirs. Subsequent inquiries seemed to confirm my neighbor's statements. The cooperative had a convoluted history. Originally, the village pastor had asked each of the 170 families then residing in Elem to contribute P50 in order to put a concrete floor into the church. Then, when those working on the project realized they needed more money to pay those hauling cement to the village, they asked for another P20 per family. When it came time to buy the cement, they asked for another P5 per family. At this point the pastor declared that it would be too expensive to floor the church with concrete, and said that the money collected should be used to buy a chainsaw. The decision was made without consulting the church members.

Other churches and individuals then contributed money to buy the saw. A portion of the income was to be kept in reserve for repairs, but, perhaps because so much of the wood was sold on credit, no cash was on hand when the saw had to be repaired. One church member reported giving money to repair the saw, but did not know if his contribution was used for that purpose.

Problems deepened when the Manobo church association began applying for land rights. The pastor and other land rights leaders borrowed funds from the cooperative to carry petitions and applications to government offices and to finance the required land surveys. None of the money borrowed was returned. When members saw the cooperative funds leaking away, they asked for the return of their investment, but the cash on hand was inadequate to meet the cooperative's obligations. The operator ended up using P11,000 of his own money to recompense some of the members. Many received nothing.

Several aspects stand out in this account of the cooperative. First and foremost is that the cooperative came to an end because of the violation of its members' trust: they asked for their money back when they perceived it was being mishandled. The funds were being handled in a manner consistent with an Individualist or Big Man society. Decisions were made by one person who had charismatic appeal but no permanent authority. If group members disagreed with him, they were free to withdraw their support (and property) and leave the group. At the same time, there were no mechanisms in place for imposing sanctions on members who violated the group's norms; withdrawal was the only recourse. Also noteworthy is the lack of transparency: decisions were made without either consulting or informing the members. There was seldom even any reporting to members of how much money the cooperative had, nor of how much was owed it.

Belanga women's group

There is one final type of cooperative group among the Manobo worthy of note: women's groups. Most of these have confined themselves to facilitating the adoption of gardening by their members, but the women's group in Belanga has had a wider focus. The group began in 1987 by growing and selling yam greens and green onions to its members. They used the proceeds to buy table sugar in the market and resell it in the village, constantly reinvesting and building up the store's capital. When the proceeds had accumulated, the group decided to improve on their water situation. At that time, the people in Belanga carried all their drinking water from springs some distance from the village. The women's group therefore decided to buy seven metal drums to collect rainwater. An outbreak of cholera later motivated the village to make the closest spring less susceptible to contamination. They obtained some contributions of funds, material, and technical input from the Philippine government and SIL, but also invested their own resources. The women gave P1,000 for cement and used hammers to break stones into gravel as contributions toward a concrete wall to protect the spring. Still later, after amassing more funds, the group bought a hand-powered grinder for P1,500. They have also raised cassava and other crops to feed their members while working on projects, and have constructed their own meeting shed.[11]

---

[11] The success of the Belanga women's group may lead us to ask whether Manobo women are more successful at managing cooperative projects. However, a review of the previous accounts shows that there were women's groups that produced no results other than promoting gardening, and that there were successful cooperative ventures that were not managed solely by women. The more important factor seems to be village cohesion. Belanga and Mayul appear to be more cohesive

Dynamics of group efficacy

In this chapter, we are examining the processes leading to political resistance and the factors affecting the effectiveness of groups making these efforts, referring to the experiences of the Manobo as a particular case in point. Having a large number of case studies would improve the certainty of any conclusions reached, yet the number of groups among the Manobo seeking land rights is limited. However, the Manobo's land rights efforts have their roots in a number of civil associations. Furthermore, as these associations are in less-direct political confrontation with outside forces, they may more accurately reflect the dynamics of group activity that are common in Manobo society. We therefore examined several kinds of Manobo civil associations.

One thing that stands out in these case studies is the Manobo's continued interest in appropriating the advantages of permanent groups. The Manobo's decision to form the AMBCI, the Tiruray's decision to form their own church association, the Manobo's continued interest in cooperative stores (despite their frequent failure), and Elem's interest in returning to a community-owned clinic (despite the partial success of privatized clinics), all demonstrate the Manobo and Tiruray peoples' continued interest in obtaining the benefits of coordination.

However, coordination comes with a price, namely, the surrender of some degree of individual autonomy to the corporate group. Prior to the intrusion of the central government and the arrival of settlers and the logging company, the Manobo could attain their desires through engaging in temporary cooperation for a limited and specific purpose. In Mary Douglas' terms, they had an Individualist society. It appears the Manobo have maintained a preference for this type of social organization, even as they are attracted to the benefits of greater internal group cohesion. Hence, among the Manobo, groups that rely on vertical coordination (giving authority to supervisors, or expecting rules to be respected and followed) or horizontal coordination (expecting the group to successfully pressure members to subordinate their personal ambitions to those of the group) have proven likely to disintegrate and fail to attain their aim. The collapse of most of Elem's cooperative stores and its chainsaw cooperative, the failure of its village-owned clinic to maintain either medicine or funds, and the conversion of its clinic pig project from providing "health insurance" to simply providing another source of income, all point to the lack of mechanisms in traditional Manobo society for maintaining sustained cooperation. However, the positive outcomes of the agricultural extension program, fruit tree acquisition effort, and privatization of the Elem clinic, demonstrate that group efforts

---

villages than Elem—in part because of size, and in part because of village history (cf. pp. 73–74).

in an Individualist society can be effective when they are designed to allow for temporary cooperation.

While some degree of cooperation is possible without horizontal or vertical coordination, our review of Manobo civil associations also points to a growing emergence of both hierarchy and group cohesion. Some of this increased coordination has been within communities. However, the two church associations provide substantial links between communities, and the Elem chainsaw cooperative attempted to facilitate the creation of similar cooperatives in two other localities. Given the Manobo's tendency to utilize Individualist social organization, group efforts among them are likely to be more effective if they do not depend on hierarchy or group solidarity. At the same time, the Manobo can expect to be able to make increasing use of these qualities to achieve their aims in the future.

7

The Tree Grows: Resistance Continues 1995–2006

Developments in political resistance

We now return to the development of political resistance among the Manobo. We saw in chapter 5 how the Manobo's political resistance and pursuit of land rights started with the Manobo church, beginning with its incorporation as the AMBCI and culminating in the AMBCI's petition for a Certificate of Ancestral Domain Claim (CADC) in 1993. DENR and PAFID, though, counseled that the petition be made through a secular organization. The Manobo land-rights leaders, many of whom are pastors, also favored this approach so that the Association could continue its other ministries even should the Manobo's opponents succeed in destroying the organization pursuing their land rights. DENR and PAFID also recommended they form a separate organization for each municipality, so that an obstruction in one municipality would not prevent the CADC from proceeding in the others. Thus, in September 1995, the Manobo and Tiruray formed five different organizations: the Tribal Community of Kalamansig Association, Tribal Community of Lebak Association, Tribal Community of Esperanza Association, Dulangan Community of Sen. Ninoy Aquino Association, and Timuay Community of Palimbang Association.[1] The leaders consisted of

---

[1] *Timuay* is a Tiruray word referring to one of two kinds of traditional leader, the other being a *képéduwan*. The Manobo *datù* and Tiruray *képéduwan* were primarily

traditional leaders (*datù* or *sulutan*), pastors, people who had held positions in ministries of the AMBCI or ATBCI, and some who were simply regarded as leading citizens. The roster of leaders demonstrated a wide network of relationships among the Manobo as well as the absence of any deep schisms between traditional, religious, and emerging leaders.

While the Manobo pursued land rights through official channels, action by the government continued at a slow pace. It will be recalled from chapter 5 that the government had sent a fact-finding mission in 1994 to investigate reports the Manobo had filed regarding abuse by the logging company. The team made no conclusive findings at that time, so the government sent a second "Fact Finding Team" in 1995 to follow up the investigation. "Provincial dialogs" were held in three municipalities, to allow locals to testify to the team. However, despite considerable testimony being given, the team made no recommendation to pursue charges. It did recommend that DENR grant a CADC to the indigenous peoples of Sultan Kudarat province. DENR, however, failed to act on that recommendation. The Manobo felt that the government had ignored their peaceful efforts to secure land rights.

At the same time, the company's abuses continued. In 1996, the company cut down 3,000 coffee trees belonging to one Manobo man and replaced them with coffee trees of its own, without either consulting with or informing the owner. The Manobo had planted the trees three years earlier on land within the Manobo's ancestral area, and they were just beginning to bear a reasonable crop.

Despite this discouragement, the Manobo continued to pursue secure tenure for their ancestral lands. In June 1996, the Tribal Community of Esperanza Association requested a CADC to cover 20,000 ha. The municipal council and Provincial Special Task Force on Ancestral Domain government supported that request and endorsed it to DENR's provincial office, which in turn forwarded it to DENR's national office. In July, DENR's regional office directed the provincial office to delineate the CADC area immediately.

The next year, 1997, saw further progress with the passage of the Indigenous Peoples Rights Act (IPRA), which was intended to grant greater legal protection to the Philippines' indigenous populations. DENR also surveyed the boundary between Maguindanao Province and that portion of the CADC adjoining it. However, other events led the Manobo to question whether any genuine progress was being made. After IPRA was passed, DENR's national under-secretary called a meeting which some of the Manobo leaders attended; however, when the leaders attempted to submit several documents to DENR, the agency refused to accept them, saying that they lacked documentary stamps. Public dialogues between

---

arbitrators, while the *timuay* had the power to command and to make binding decisions. See Schlegel (1970:58–68) for a detailed description of the *képéduwan* and *timuay*.

the government, Manobo and Tiruray populace, and M&S Co. followed in Esperanza and Isulan. The Manobo were initially encouraged to receive a hearing, but soon afterward some of the leaders began hearing that the company was seeking to kill them. The head of the national Commission on Human Rights reportedly told them he would take their case to the National Bureau of Investigation, but the leaders observed no results.

The next year, 1998, saw a continuation of progress and obstacle. The Department of Environment and Natural Resources, it will be recalled, had halted M&S Co. from logging in 1994 (p. 84). However, in 1998, Manobo leaders learned that the mayors of four of the five municipalities in which they live had signed a letter from M&S Co. to DENR asking permission to resume logging. That year, though, was also an election year, and the politicians actively courted the Manobo vote, with several candidates visiting both Elem and Danu.

Two years later it was much the same. Datù Éyét Énggéw, a prominent Manobo leader in the Kulaman area, was killed in an incident that many Manobo believe was deliberate.[2] However, the Manobo did make limited political gains. In 2001, six of Salangsang's seven *barangay* councilors were Manobo. Further, the Manobo were courted by the local politicians, with several candidates visiting Elem. The Manobo were also undeterred in addressing officials. In January, an assortment of Manobo emerging, traditional, and church leaders from the Elem area petitioned Sultan Kudarat Gov. Pax Mangudadatu for the construction of a drinking water system for the "tribal *barangay*" to be created by Philippine House Bill 2540 (submitted in August 1996). In September of that same year, and again the following January, the heads of the five municipal land rights organizations, plus several *datù* and AMBCI officials, wrote to Gov. Mangudadatu requesting him to attend a "General Conference of Tribal Communities" to discuss the formation of Manobo-controlled municipalities and *barangay*. The governor neither responded nor attended the meeting, yet the Manobo's continued efforts to communicate with him and other officials indicated a persistent and coordinated political will.

Developments in 2003 suggest soft commitment from government agencies to the Manobo. An April memorandum from DENR's national office to its regional directors specified they suspend the issuance of any new licenses within areas covered by CADC applications unless they first consulted with the NCIP and obtained the explicit permission of the indigenous

---

[2] According to the Manobo, an unidentified government office requested their community leaders in the Kulaman area to attend a meeting in the municipality, offering them remuneration to attend and arranging for free transportation to the meeting in the back of a private dump truck. The driver ostensibly lost control of the vehicle, which rolled and crushed many of the passengers. Four, including one *datù*, died at the scene; Datù Éyét died later, never recovering. However, the driver fled, unhurt.

communities that would be affected, and report on any such licenses already issued, implying that the agency had been issuing licenses within areas legally committed to indigenous communities. Guidelines issued by the NCIP in October 2003, spelling out how the NCIP intended to implement IPRA, likewise suggest a soft commitment to the indigenous peoples. Fewer than half the members of the agency's national and regional-level committees were to come from indigenous peoples' organizations (POs), keeping control firmly in the government's hands (see chapter 5, footnote 6). Indigenous representation at the provincial level was somewhat greater, but the chairman was to be selected from government-appointed NCIP officials, thus leaving the government in effective control of provincial-level decisions. The government seemed to be reluctant to cede any real power to the indigenous peoples, including the Manobo.

Despite the government's weak commitment, the Manobo and Tiruray saw some progress on land rights in 2003. The Tribal Community of Esperanza Association (TCEA) applied for a CADT (Certificate of Ancestral Domain Title), to replace the earlier CADC (Certificate of Ancestral Domain Claim). The Provincial Special Task Force on Ancestral Domain visited the area in January 2004 to conduct an on-site investigation and issued a report substantiating the TCEA's CADT application.

My informants among the Manobo and Tiruray report that in March 2005, M&S Co. agreed in a meeting with Manobo leaders and government officials that the government could proceed to survey the CADT area for its delineation. However, armed company guards soon obstructed the survey, and the survey team acquiesced, as they had only one rifle. (The team later claimed they stopped because of an order from DENR.) Within two months a public "dialogue" meeting accused M&S Co. of stopping the survey. However, when the NCIP regional director questioned M&S Co.'s managers, they denied the accusation. In response, the NCIP's Provincial Consultative Body wrote NCIP's national chairman, requesting action on the Manobo's behalf. This was followed by a meeting of several indigenous POs in Davao in April (cf. p. 120) in which the representatives of several POs and NGOs signed a letter asking the government to cancel M&S Co.'s IFMAs in Sultan Kudarat. The survey was attempted again in May after a new work order from NCIP's national chairman, but obstructed once again by company guards.

The government's delay in response led the Manobo to take further steps in late 2005. Philippine President Gloria Macapagal Arroyo had proposed amending the national constitution to allow a president to be elected to a subsequent term, a proposal that Filipinos referred to as the "cha cha" (charter change). The NCIP's headquarters were evidently concerned that rights extended to the indigenous peoples under the previous president, Fidel Ramos, might be rolled back should the charter change be approved. Thus, in late 2005, the NCIP convened a meeting of Provincial Consultative Body

(PCB) chairmen, intended to put pressure on the administration to keep reforms initiated under President Ramos, even should the "cha cha" pass.[3] One result was that the Manobo and Tiruray elected officers for their own PCB, thereby forming a new organization that could pursue their land rights.

The opportunity for action arose a year later, when M&S Co. obstructed the survey for the CADC in Esperanza. The PCB decided that if the survey for Esperanza went ahead, they would then ask for the survey to proceed for the remainder of Manobo and Tiruray territory in the other four municipalities. They would ask for the NCIP commissioner to sign a statement saying that the survey would be done by a particular time, so that they could hold the government to its commitment. If the Esperanza survey did not go through, they would then request that M&S Co.'s agreement with the government—its Industrial Forestry Management Area—be cancelled.

By late 2005, some of the land rights leaders had reportedly decided that if their latest appeal to the government produced no results that they would consider turning to violence, meeting force with force. However, cooler heads prevailed at a meeting of land rights leaders and traditional leaders shortly thereafter, and they decided they would petition the government to rescind its agreements with the company. The petition was to be endorsed by the traditional leaders and the several land rights organizations and signed by the Manobo and Tiruray population at large. Significantly, the group also decided how they would collect and handle contributions to support the petition effort.

One factor that stands out in the Manobo's interactions with the Philippine state is that the government is not monolithic: it is comprised of many offices and agencies, some of which are more responsive to the Manobo than others. The Department of Defense appears to be among the more responsive parties. In March 2004, the Department of Defense went to the municipal land rights associations and informed them that the Manobo and Tiruray could apply to have "cultural guards." The guards would be trained and paid by the government,[4] and would patrol their ancestral domain once it was granted.[5] There is also evidence that local government is becoming more responsive. There are now elected Manobo and Tiruray officials, and in 2005, fully six of Salangsang's seven *barangay* councilors were indigenous peoples; three were Manobo, and three Tiruray. In contrast, though, DENR seems to be more responsive to well-funded exploiters of natural resources than to the indigenous peoples.

---

[3] The Provincial Consultative Bodies were formed by the NCIP.

[4] There is a long history of government-affiliated community militias in the Philippines, including the CHDF (Civil Home Defense Force), CAFGU (Civilian Armed Forces Geographical Unit), and now-active CVO (Civil Voluntary Organization).

[5] The Manobo have selected several men to be guards, but by October 2006 training had not begun.

Changes between administrations, and changes in law, create additional ambiguity. The Indigenous Peoples Rights Act (IPRA), passed in 1997, stated that once the government announced its intent to establish a CADT in a newspaper, it must investigate the veracity of the claim within fifteen days and then issue the CADT. However, the law did not address the older CADCs that the CADT had replaced. It also established a conflict in jurisdiction between the NCIP and the Land Registration Authority over the legal requirements for surveys, which has prevented the implementation of several CADTs. The change in administration when Gloria Macapagal Arroyo took over the presidency from Joseph Estrada at the beginning of 2001 has created additional problems. President Arroyo claimed that many CADTs approved in Estrada's last days in office were fraudulent and overturned all CADTs awarded, including those that were legitimate. For all these reasons, the Manobo's CADTs are currently stalled in internal government conflicts.

The Manobo are divided in their reaction to their current situation. Many feel they cannot resist because of overwhelming force, as one man expressed:

> "Now, our place has been filled up with gmelina [a plantation timber species], but we don't take revenge, because we are unable. We cannot resist their weapons. We don't fight back, so that our children and wives are not hurt. We trust ourselves to Jesus, so don't fight back. If you fight back, you'll die. Because we don't fight back, we now have no land."

Others, however, appear increasingly tempted to take up arms. Even those eschewing violence are increasingly frustrated with the government's lack of action on their behalf. As one leader expressed:

> "What can we do to complain to the government? If we complain, they don't pay attention. We don't have money to go to Isulan. When election time comes, they give us a little dried fish. When the mayor or BC [*barangay* captain] we've supported wins the election and we go to him for help, we don't get any. So, forget about that."

Despite reservations about the government's responsiveness, the Manobo submitted a request through a newly formed land-rights organization, the Sagip Fusaka Inged, on 19 June 2006, asking that M&S Co. agreements with the government be cancelled.[6] They delivered their petition to the Office of the President, the national offices of the National Commission on Indigenous Peoples, the Philippine Commission on Human Rights, and the Department of Environment and Natural Resources, as well as the office of Congressman Teng Mangudadatu, who represents Sultan Kudarat Province. The submission reportedly infuriated the logging company. However, the

---

[6] The Sagip Fusaka Inged is an umbrella organization that was created in 2005 to unite the five organizations the Manobo and Tiruray formed in 1995 to pursue their land rights (cf. pp. 84–85). Another umbrella organization, the *Duma Pelikù Ka* Federation, had been formed for the same purpose in or somewhat before 1999, but had become inactive.

Manobo apparently received a sympathetic hearing from NCIP Chairman Janet Serrano and President Arroyo, who reportedly committed to seeing that the company's concession agreements are overturned.

The passage of the UN Declaration on the Rights of Indigenous Peoples may signal growing responsiveness to the Manobo's concerns. The Philippine government was one of the nations that voted in favor of the Declaration, which was finally adopted on 13 September 2007 after 22 years of debate by the UN General Assembly. This was a positive step for indigenous peoples everywhere. As Richard Clemmer (2009) stated, "With the UN General Assembly's passage of the Declaration on the Rights of Indigenous Peoples... deprivation of indigenous peoples' resources has become an internationally actionable offense." The Declaration is a promising document; how much it changes the Manobo's situation remains to be seen.

Coordination in the Manobo's pursuit of land rights

While the Manobo and Tiruray have clearly employed cooperation in their pursuit of land rights, the bodies they have formed for that purpose display ambiguity in their degree of organization. The Manobo and Tiruray formed a single organization, the *Duma Pelikù Ka* Federation, to reunite the Manobo and Tiruray into one organization seeking their land rights. The leaders of the five municipal land rights organizations followed this with a resolution, addressed to the local governor and congressman, to unite the Manobo villages of Sultan Kudarat into a single municipality. It is evident that the Manobo were seeking the formation of a single, larger entity that they envisioned would be more effective in achieving their rights. At same time, the various land rights organizations were having trouble raising the funds needed to pursue land rights. The leaders of one of the municipal organizations sent a letter to several villages in 1995, asking each family to contribute P150 (approximately three days' wages) to help them pursue the group's land rights. The response was minimal. In early 2006, one leader stated that the Manobo once gave small contributions to the land rights leaders when they were preparing to visit government offices, but that the leaders now had to look for funds on their own, implying they often had to meet the expenses themselves. He attributed this in part to the Manobo not understanding the need for group solidarity, and in part to the leaders' failure to render a financial account to their constituents. The Manobo's hesitancy to contribute was likely related to the similar lack of financial accountability by leaders of the Manobo church association. As with the cooperatives, lack of transparency was limiting group cohesion. In contrast, the doubt sown did not destroy the land rights organizations, likely due to the much greater urgency of obtaining land rights.

The organizations have taken actions to enhance their cohesion. One case is that of the Tribal Community of Esperanza Association, which contains a large number of constituents from both the Manobo and Tiruray.

Consequently, the leaders made a conscious effort to build unity in the group. They decided to use the word "Tribal" in their name to communicate that the Manobo and Tiruray were united as a single group, and when they selected leaders were careful to choose both elders and younger leaders. It appears that the TCEA has been able to communicate to its constituents that it is financially trustworthy. It has established two community projects (essentially cooperatives) that have provided funds for its efforts, and has also received substantial voluntary contributions. These have not been entirely sufficient for its needs, but they have enabled its officers to visit government offices in Manila. Once there, NGOs have been willing to finance their return home.

The Manobo land rights associations have also struggled with the issue of coordination with outside organizations, namely with NGOs. After their initial contact with PAFID, they have learned of and made contact with an increasing number of NGOs that are assisting indigenous groups with land rights and human rights. However, this seems to have been of limited value, as the land rights leaders relate that PAFID continues to provide them the greatest assistance with gaining land rights. Additionally, the land rights leaders have reservations about approaching some NGOs because of the groups' promoting the use of violence or abandoning the Manobo's newly acquired allegiance to Christianity.

While the Manobo land rights organizations have made limited progress in coordinating with NGOs, this has been balanced by the formation of new ties with other indigenous peoples. The Manobo joined forty other indigenous peoples to form a Mindanao-wide association, the Panagtagbo Mindanao, and later joined a nationwide consortium of indigenous people's organizations called KASAPI. In April 2005, several NGOs[7] sponsored a meeting in Davao to facilitate cooperation between Philippine indigenous peoples' organizations. The Manobo land rights leaders report that they developed several helpful contacts during the forum.

Summary

In this chapter, we have examined the processes leading to political resistance among the Manobo and have identified factors that have influenced the effectiveness of their cooperative efforts in both civil and political domains. The Manobo have demonstrated a sustained interest in appropriating the advantages of a more integrated social organization: they have formed numerous groups, none of which existed in traditional culture, for a variety of purposes, including religion, literacy, health, economic advantage, and land rights. Each of these has emerged from the ostensibly apolitical domain of religion. At the opening of this chapter, the

---

[7] Among these were Anthro Watch, PAFID, Tabang Mindanao, IPEX, KASAPI, and NTFP.

Manobo church association petitioned the Philippine government to grant the Manobo secure rights to their ancestral lands. As events unfolded, the church association turned over the pursuit of land rights to specialized secular organizations formed for that purpose, while simultaneously giving rise to a network of literacy teachers, health workers, and agricultural extension agents. These activities may have inspired the Manobo's interest in cooperative stores and lumber production groups by demonstrating the possibility of cooperation, at the same time that they provided many of the leaders for the cooperatives.

At the same time, the move to a more integrated social organization has not come easily. The Manobo church association and the land rights organizations have struggled, especially in financial matters, and many of the economic cooperatives have failed. Examination of the many action groups among the Manobo suggests several factors that may have contributed to the groups' survival and effectiveness:

Group cohesion is evidently promoted by smaller group size, ideological homogeneity, and the ability to impose sanctions on those violating group norms.

Communication between previously isolated individuals permits the development of relationships that individuals may later utilize for cooperation. This describes what happened in the entrance of the pastors into the political realm of pursuing land rights, as well as the networking of Manobo land rights leaders with those among other indigenous peoples.

Coordination between groups is promoted by the maintenance of harmonious relations between leaders in different groups and in different types of groups.

Maintaining a network over a large area will likely lead to the emergence of hierarchy (that is, to a more complex system entailing vertical as well as horizontal coordination).

One factor that appears to lead to the continued existence of a group is sheer necessity: when there is appreciable need, the advantages of group membership are more likely to outweigh the costs.

At the same time, lack of financial transparency may lead to the dissolution of the group, or at least to the reticence of members to contribute to it.

Links with sympathetic organizations (whether NGOs, POs, or GOs) may contribute to groups' effectiveness and survival, perhaps due to the provision of outside resources, including training, encouragement, and helpful contacts.

Groups are also more likely to be effective and to continue if their structure and practices parallel those currently used in the culture.

"Necessity," the saying goes, "is the mother of invention." In the case of groups, it appears that necessity promotes both their development and their continued existence. We have traced the slow incubation of increasing integration within Manobo society from the time that settlers arrived in the area to the present. Integration (and the cooperation dependent upon it), already begun with the advent of the settlers, increased even more after the arrival of the M&S logging company. The Manobo have addressed many needs, not the least of which is obtaining secure access to their ancestral lands.

While the Manobo have made remarkable progress in organizing to pursue land rights, the government has been slow in responding. The passage of the Indigenous Peoples Rights Act, and the consequent formation of the National Commission on Indigenous Peoples, are positive steps, as is the government's support for the UN Declaration on the Rights of Indigenous Peoples. However, the Manobo continue to wait for rights to their land, while they see requests from large companies being quickly approved. Their response to date has been peaceful, but there is growing frustration at the government's lack of attention to their plight.

8

A Walk through the Woods

Looking around: What have we learned?

We have been looking at the experience of a single people, the Manobo, in their interactions with those who have invaded their ancestral territory. Yet it is not an isolated study, for it brings out patterns that we can expect to see among the many other indigenous peoples who are encountering similar pressures from more powerful societies attempting to take over their ancestral domains. This close look at the land-use confrontation between the Manobo people and those taking over their ancestral domain has demonstrated connections between religion, political action, and environment that are often overlooked. In the particular case of the Manobo, an indigenous form of Christianity has provided the foundations to mobilize resources and support for the reversal of environmental degradation, as well as for the pursuit of economic well-being and social justice.

Environmental impact

Comparison of the current landscape with the forest and soil under the Manobo's traditional system clearly demonstrates that the settlers' sedentary agricultural system is not sustainable. ["Settlers" is defined in the preface.] The Manobo's accounts, plus my own observations between 1983 and 2006, indicate that the forest was once much more extensive.[1] In just the

---

[1] The tremendous loss of forest cover has been well documented for Mindanao. In 1900, 93 percent of the island's area was old-growth forest. That figure dropped

two years of 2005 and 2006, wide areas had been cut down by the logging company active in the area. Wildlife is also far less common than when I first lived among the Manobo.

The soil is also suffering. The traditional swidden system protected the soil from severe erosion and allowed it to regenerate. In contrast, the sedentary agricultural system the settlers have introduced is not suited to the pronounced slopes found in Manobo territory. Most of the land farmed by settlers has lost the topsoil, and many plots have eroded down to orange clay subsoil. Many farmers have attempted to compensate for the loss of natural fertility by using inorganic fertilizers, but have instead lost their land to pay their debts to the merchants.

Even if the Manobo are not allowed to return to the more environmentally gentle swidden system of their tradition, they have demonstrated the willingness to adopt new technologies that are more profitable and ecologically sensitive than the sedentary agricultural system they have been forced to adopt. The vast majority of farmers now grow coffee, and many are in the process of adopting fruit trees and coconuts. Some are moving from extensive to intensive agriculture, producing high-value crops (for example, green onions and cabbage) on small areas, which makes it more practical to protect the soil from erosion. Others are controlling runoff, putting limited areas into irrigated rice production and fishponds. However, lack of secure land tenure makes it difficult to invest in such measures. As in many similar situations where indigenous peoples' management systems have been overturned, the state cannot expect the adoption of land-use systems that will simultaneously preserve the environment while realizing reasonable benefits from it unless they support the Manobo in their pursuit of secure land tenure.

This study has also brought out the state's role in maintaining civil peace. Despite the prevalence of internecine violence in their past (cf. Garvan 1941), and sometimes violent altercations with the neighboring Tiruray and Tboli peoples, the Manobo have seldom exercised violence toward settlers, their brief entry into the Toothpick War being the prime exception. Yet, the state has done little to protect the Manobo or other residents of the area from violence. The state has permitted the logging company to maintain a private security force that has been reported on numerous occasions to have abused the Manobo, settlers, and Muslims. Separatist rebel groups have also threatened the Manobo and settlers. If the government fails to enforce its laws against all the parties intruding on the Manobo's territory, the Manobo could

---

to 50 percent during the 1950s, when Philippine President Ramón Magsaysay launched a huge resettlement effort for millions of landless Filipinos from the central and northern portions of the country, and has now declined to less than 3 percent (Sohmer 1992:53; Hires and Headland 1977). Over that same period, the national population rose from 7.7 million in 1903 (Early and Headland 1998:32) to 103 million today (Population Reference Bureau 2015).

resort to violence, as have indigenous peoples in the Mexican state of Oaxaca, to name just one prominent altercation in the recent past.

Emergence of resistance from religion and civil associations

External pressures on a society frequently lead to new religious movements, as seen in the histories of the cargo cults, the Kiowa Ghost Dance (Kracht 1992), and other millenary movements (Kapferer 1997:324–325). We have seen how the Manobo and nearby Tiruray people have mobilized religious dynamics in their response, which entailed a surprisingly rapid and widespread acceptance of Protestant Christianity, as well as lesser interest in shamanistic millenary movements. (Their lack of interest in the latter may be the result of having experienced pronounced defeat at the hands of the settlers and Philippine government, making a less militant ideology appear more practical.) Significantly, the Manobo embrace of Protestant Christianity—which in some ways parallels the response of African Americans in the United States—laid the foundation for an ever-increasing network of relationships within Manobo society, as previously isolated individuals made contact through pastors' meetings and began to pursue common interests. The churches' subsequent involvement in literacy, health, and agricultural development greatly expanded this network. Hence, there was a ready web of civil relationships in place that the Manobo could turn to when they decided to actively pursue rights to their ancestral lands.

The progression from religious roots to economic development to political mobilization is consistent with the theory of social capital, in which civil associations provide the foundation for political resistance. However, the process among the Manobo was not merely a progression from civil associations to political action, due to the unique dynamics played by religion. For the Manobo, the adoption of Christianity and the consequent meeting of pastors with one another resulted in a network of relationships absent in the traditional religion. Furthermore, the "this-worldly" as well as "other-worldly" focus of religion among the Manobo resulted in the pastors addressing a multitude of needs: health, literacy, agricultural development, and land rights, as well as more "traditional" functions such as conflict settlement, marriage counseling, and moral instruction. Some pastors took on some of the new roles, but there was also a proliferation of other new-type community leaders. This spawned an even broader network of leaders among the Manobo. This network included the *datù*, as there was no conflict between the *datù* and the pastors, and thus none with the new leaders that came from the church. Thus, the network of relationships, plus the "natural" involvement of the pastors in land rights, provided a ready social base to mobilize resources and support for pursuing land rights.

The process by which political resistance developed among the Manobo from religious roots is also theoretically significant in highlighting the inadequacy of restricting the terms "subjugation," "adaptation," and "resistance" to the political domain. Interaction with an outside society may result in changes not only to a people's political system, but also to their economic practices (for example, property right regimes), livelihood practices (for example, agricultural technology), and religion (for example, emergence of millenarian movements). Societies actively respond to pressures upon them in many different domains. By labeling such response "resistance" only when it occurs in the political realm, we overlook the fact that groups may learn to resist in one area and then go on to resist in the area of politics. It therefore seems more accurate to label all active response as "resistance," especially in cases where resistance in one domain leads to resistance in the political realm.

Basic to the role played by religion in mobilizing political resistance among the Manobo is their understanding of religion being at least as pertinent to this world as to the next. Traditional Manobo religion was concerned mostly with healing—that is, with maintaining harmonious relations between humans and the spirits that can cause sickness. When the Manobo adopted Christianity, healing and a concern for whatever affects well-being in this world remained primary foci of religion. It was therefore natural for the pastors to address health and economic concerns, which led to the training of health workers, the establishment of clinics, and the training of agricultural extension workers. This in turn led to the establishment of economic cooperatives in several villages. This, too, should not be surprising. Close association between religious, political, and social welfare movements parallels developments in the Protestant Reformation, Roman Catholic peasant movements in Latin America, and modern developments in Islam from Africa to Indonesia. The Protestant Reformation, for instance, was noted for the promotion of literacy and education among commoners, while Catholic peasant movements in Latin America frequently include an emphasis on making health care available to the poor. Islamic communities also contribute to the poor among them, redistributing funds from the religiously-mandated alms (*zakat*) collected from practitioners.

The involvement of religion in mobilizing political action should not be surprising. Contrary to its frequent dismissal as "the opiate of the masses," religion has played a significant part in mobilizing resistance in many well-known political movements, including the African-American civil rights movement (for example, Rev. Dr. Martin Luther King Jr., Rev. Al Sharpton, and Rev. Jesse Jackson), Mohandas Gandhi's struggle for Indian independence, and contemporary Sunni and Shiite movements in the Middle East.[2] We can expect that

---

[2] Note that the intersection of the religious and political domains does not inherently produce either violence or peace. Christianity, for instance, has sometimes stimulated aggression, as in the Hundred Year's War between France and England and the religious wars during the Protestant Reformation, but it has also produced the pacifist Mennonites and the nonviolent resistance of Rev. Dr. Martin Luther King Jr.

among other indigenous peoples as well, civil relationships will be used to mobilize resources and support for the pursuit of political objectives, including the quest for land rights.

Evolution of sociopolitical integration

This investigation into the history of the Manobo people and their activity groups has demonstrated another process important to the land-rights efforts of other indigenous peoples, namely, a gradual evolution in the complexity of internal organization. We have seen how the intrusion of outside political forces and populations initially undermined the local society's political structures—that is, the traditional *datù* system—due to the expansion of the central government as settlers gained increasing control over the area, consolidated by the Philippine government's military defeat of a Manobo "rebellion" in the 1970s. However, the pastors' subsequent involvement with physical and economic needs, and then with land rights, led to a growing network of relationships throughout the society. Moreover, this network was not simply a mass of contacts, as social capital theory may sometimes suggest. There was an evolution of development of both peer-to-peer and superior-inferior relationships: evolution from individualist toward both collectivist and hierarchical organizational structures. The Manobo developed increasing levels of internal coordination, in direct response to the needs the invasion had brought about. There have been many factors contributing to their need: the government's failure to recognize rights to their ancestral land; the awarding of logging concessions; the logging company's aggressive efforts to remove Manobo populations and prevent them from pursuing traditional agricultural systems, and destruction of Manobo crops and houses; settlers' seizure of Manobo land; and inability to compete economically with the settlers. Yet, after the initial traumatic undermining of the traditional political system, the Manobo appear to have responded to these pressures through an alternative strategy of increased internal organization—an adaptive response anticipated by the work of Adams, Rambo, Poggie, and Singelis et al. Their work suggests that pressures from outside are crucial in stimulating the development of internal organization. Examples of such pressures include the following:

- The Philippine government and society are suspicious of unofficial groups, producing pressure on the Manobo church association to legally incorporate. Compliance with the requirements for incorporation forced the association to adopt a board of directors, thereby moving the group toward greater centralization.
- A desire to keep free of government suspicion, and to have a better opportunity to seek assistance, put strong pressure on the literacy and health workers to have representatives to the government, thereby leading to the appointment of literacy and health supervisors, with the

consequent move to greater centralization.
* The literacy and health workers' dependence on a limited number of outside specialists for training, funding, supplies, and representation to government likewise made supervisors a necessity, again leading to greater centralization.
* The Manobo's increased contact with a market economy led to an increased demand for market products. At the same time, their distance from major towns, where goods are available at much less cost and where their own produce commands a higher price than in the mountains, led to a desire on their part to eliminate the middlemen. These two factors together produced an interest in forming cooperatives for both buying and selling.
* Finally, the need for secure land tenure, never an issue before the intrusion of settlers and loggers, has led to far more cooperation than at any time in the past—not only at the village or regional level, but indeed throughout the entire language group.

Group effectiveness: Obstacles to the evolution of sociopolitical integration

Consideration of the process by which sociopolitical integration has increased among the Manobo also sheds light on the difficulties that some of their activity groups have experienced. As the work of Lansing and de Vet (1999), Rambo (1991b), Poggie (1995), and Singelis et al. (1995) brings out, while cooperation enables participants to mobilize more resources toward their aims than is possible for the individual household, the necessary coordination comes at a cost. Coordination requires the surrender of some measure of individual control over resources and decisions to the group or its authorities. However, groups are rarely homogeneous, and individuals may disagree as to whether the benefits of cooperation are worth the personal cost. Individuals may also be personally undecided, and therefore ambivalent in their commitment to the group. Mishandling of group-controlled resources and the suspicion thereby aroused thus poses a direct threat to group cohesion. The histories of the several action groups examined in this study strongly suggest that lack of financial transparency may lead to the dissolution of the group, or at least to the reticence of members to contribute to it—a phenomenon mirrored in the myriad accounts of cooperatives that have collapsed elsewhere.

Rambo's work indicates that individuals are more willing to surrender individual rights to the group when they face significant need. It is therefore not surprising that while financial misconduct has destroyed cooperative stores, it has merely made it difficult for the land rights organizations to obtain contributions; it has not destroyed them. That partial immunity to collapse is encouraging. But at the same time, the land rights groups will likely become more effective if they adopt practices for financial transparency. (Financial transparency may also be advantageous in obtaining outside funding. Like many other developing nations, the Philippine state has a distinctly limited budget, and is therefore not a reliable source of funds for the Manobo's needs. Nongovernmental organizations may be willing to provide finding, but only if they see evidence of financial responsibility. Manobo organizations will have to establish mechanisms for financial transparency, and demonstrate that they are utilizing them, before they can expect to obtain outside funding. The same principle would apply to action groups in other cultures as well.)

Another factor contributing to cooperation within a society—and by extension, to the achievement of widely held goals—is the maintenance of harmonious relations between leaders in different groups (and different types of groups). The lack of infighting among *datù*, pastors, Manobo government officials, literacy workers, and health workers has undoubtedly allowed the Manobo to channel more resources and energy into the pursuit of land rights than would otherwise have been possible.

Consideration of the various activity groups among the Manobo also makes clear that the structures and practices they have employed for collective action are heavily influenced by preexisting traditional patterns, particularly those derived from the individualist way of life and economic precedents such as the *kepesagud* practice (the arrangement for dividing returns between an animal's owner and caretaker). The value of designing programs to "fit" traditional patterns was attested to by the outcomes of the fruit tree program, Elem clinic, and agricultural extension program. At the same time, the Manobo land-rights organizations (and the church association with its associated literacy, health, and agricultural development programs) are moving toward greater hierarchy and far greater organizational complexity than anything that existed in the traditional culture. It appears that the "best practice" for action groups may be to accommodate their structure and practices to traditional cultural patterns, while simultaneously working toward forms that permit greater cooperation.

Finally, while the environmental invasions of the Manobo's ancestral domain have clearly wreaked havoc, it is also evident that not all outside contact is detrimental. The decades-long involvement of SIL and TAP, providing training to indigenous groups without exercising control over them, has played a demonstrable role in facilitating the emergence and maturation of activity groups among the Manobo. PAFID has played a similar role more recently. This is not to say that all NGOs are alike: there is a wide variety of non-governmental organizations, differing in both commitment and agenda. Similarly, government officials—even within the same institution—have also varied in how they have interacted with the Manobo. While the intrusion of the state has had a serious negative impact on the Manobo, some officials have provided justice and protection to the Manobo, while others have provided access to inexpensive agricultural materials and medical care. Indigenous groups can benefit from cooperation with outside groups, so long as they exercise discernment.

Listening: What does it mean?

Research studies often conclude with recommendations, and those recommendations are often directed to "the powers that be"—usually considered to be the national government, and occasionally foreign governments or international lending institutions. Yet it is worth asking who, indeed, possesses power. It is evident that the logging company wields tremendous influence. It is also evident that the government does as well—note that the government halted the company's logging, but also created the situation that encourages the company's abuse of the Manobo. We have also seen in preceding chapters that the Manobo, despite their apparent powerlessness, have exerted genuine influence upon the government and, through it, upon the logging company. In recognition, then, that there are many parties with power to affect the well-being of all in the area, I will address my recommendations to each of the stakeholders involved: the Manobo themselves, M&S Co., the numerous local and national government offices and agencies having jurisdiction over the Manobo, and the NGOs assisting the Manobo.

To government offices and agencies

The pressures exerted by outside forces on the Manobo have produced an array of civil associations, which have in turn given rise to organizations devoted to obtaining secure access to the land of their ancestors. Despite the sometimes fraudulent and violent loss of their land, the Manobo have responded peaceably. However, continued denial of their claims is leading to frustration, raising the specter of the same kind of violence that has plagued other parts of the Philippines. The passage of IPRA is a commendable step, as is the government's signing of the UN Declaration on the Rights of Indigenous Peoples, so long as those resolutions are enforced. Devolution is another commendable step, placing decisions where the best information is and where the persons most affected reside. In keeping with the spirit of both devolution and IPRA, I would urge the government to grant the Manobo full authority over their ancestral territory. If the Manobo are allowed to determine their own future, we can expect they will not only provide for their own needs, but also responsibly care for the natural resources of their territory and become significant contributors to national prosperity.

To M&S Co.

I have used the term "resistance" because of its popularity in the academic literature, but could readily substitute the terms "empowerment," "self-determination," or "taking civic responsibility." While the Manobo have learned to "resist" the incursions into their ancestral territory, that resistance has been peaceful. My conversations with numerous leaders among them suggest that they remain well inclined to act as good neighbors toward those around them. However, the maintenance of good relations requires reciprocity among neighbors. Dissolution of the company's security force and cooperation with the government's efforts to grant the Manobo secure access to that small portion of their ancestral lands not yet titled to settlers would do much to create an environment where all parties can pursue a harmonious and prosperous future.

To NGOs (and concerned GOs)

Efforts to assist indigenous peoples are more likely to succeed if those from outside follow the local "rules of the game"—that is, if they work within both the traditional and the emerging culture. Groups among Manobo designed for individualist social organization work well. However, they are limited in what they can accomplish, as greater coordination is required for more effectiveness. While such coordination requires skills and attitudes not currently prevalent, the Manobo are demonstrating increasing levels of horizontal and vertical coordination. It will take time for the perceived benefit of coordination to exceed its perceived cost. It may be possible to facilitate the Manobo's adoption of greater coordination by providing training in skills that prevent loss of trust, namely, in record-keeping and in reporting to the group.

To the Manobo

Manobo society has not disintegrated. Rather, the Manobo have changed their social organization to respond to the new pressures they are facing, in many cases with notable results. The many groups they have created for cooperation attest to an interest in appropriating the advantages of greater internal coordination. At the same time, the dissolution of several groups formed for economic cooperation, and the financial difficulties experienced by the land-rights groups and church association, suggest that adopting new forms of social organization must be accompanied by a willingness to "pay the costs" inherent in those forms. As with NGOs, the greatest effectiveness will likely come from working within current culture while working toward the new forms desired. Particular attention should be paid to identifying and following practices that will ensure financial transparency, thereby maintaining the trust necessary for groups to continue.

To researchers

A final word is due to researchers regarding methods, theory, and additional research needs. The in-depth study of a single society has proven useful in elucidating the processes by which a society modifies its social organization to respond to invasions of its resource base. Large-scale surveys of the

entire population, had they been done, may have yielded useful quantitative data, but would have yielded considerably less insight into the interaction of groups and external forces, and into the evolution of the groups'
internal organization, both of which can only be determined by examining
the history of specific groups. Using a modified snowball approach, it was
possible to quickly develop a complete inventory of the activity groups in
the research area, and to then interview focus groups comprised of a high
percentage of the groups' members. A focus on activities also provided a
ready springboard for inquiry into norms and attitudes, while avoiding the
idealized answers often given to direct questions of a hypothetical nature.

Regarding theoretical paradigms, quantitative analyses of the relationships between and within groups (namely, ethnographic linear programming, and computer modeling of ecosystems) provided useful insights into
relationships, but paradigms that focused on social relationships, and particularly on the emergence and exercise of power, were more useful in
elucidating the processes by which the Manobo have responded to the new
pressures they are facing. Social capital theory was useful in drawing attention to the foundational role played by prior relationships in mobilizing
political resistance, but is inadequate by itself, as it focuses only on the
gross occurrence of relationships rather than on their nature, configuration, and evolution. Grid-group theory (pp. 6-9), research on the mechanisms by which vertical and horizontal relationships emerge in response to
outside pressures (pp. 14–15), and studies of cultural evolution focused on
social forces (p. 13) provided the paradigms for analyzing the development
of social organization and corollary resistance among the Manobo. (The
more recent theory of political ecology likewise places emphasis on the
relationship between external forces and internal reconfigurations, both in
the social system and the interaction between society and environment. It
also emphasizes the phenomenon of "scale," the level at which interaction
is taking place, thereby helping to ensure that local, regional, and national
forces are all taken into account. Political ecology also acknowledges the
internal workings of a society under the rubric of "agency." However, the
paradigms I have relied on are more explicit in their focus on the specific
processes by which social organization evolves, so were more useful for
my purposes.) Common property regime (CPR) theory (pp. 17–18) provided
additional detail for analysis of the relationship between a group's internal
organization and its practices for resource management.

This study of the Manobo has explored the impact of environmental invasions of their homeland on their social organization, and traced the processes by which they modified their social organization to respond to these
invasions. Certain trends have been evident among the Manobo, including
the stimulation of internal coordination by an adverse political climate, the
importance of civil institutions, the role that religion can play in facilitating civil and political institutions, and the increase in effectiveness possible

through deliberate accommodation to existing structures and practices. Each of these findings is substantiated by previous studies based on the theories I have employed, strongly suggesting that we can expect to see many of these same trends manifested among other indigenous peoples dealing with the invasion of their territory. In this regard, this study achieved my goal of elucidating the processes at work among the Manobo and helping to make clearer the possibilities at hand for them and other indigenous peoples. At the same time, a full understanding of the processes by which indigenous populations change their "cultural tools" to respond to new pressures can only come from the comparison of widely differing cases of environmental invasions. Thus, this study is also a call to researchers to conduct similar studies among and between other peoples, to the end that indigenous peoples worldwide will become better equipped in their quest to form just and harmonious relationships with their neighbors.

9

Epilogue

My study of the Manobo, and of the social changes they have made to respond to the invasions of their homeland, was completed in 2006, but the Manobo's story continues. Since that time, they have formed at least one new organization, Kiduma, to pursue their rights to their ancestral territory. On 30 April 2015, a spokesman for Kiduma, John Calaba, disappeared while visiting the outpost of a militia sponsored by the logging company. He has not been seen since, and observers believe he was killed by the militia (Capistrano 2015; Dulce 2015; Froese 2015).

The Manobo have been peacefully seeking rights to a small portion of their ancestral territory since 1993, and continue to seek harmonious relations with their neighbors. Whether that goal can be achieved remains an open question, to be answered in large part by those who consider themselves powerful. The Manobo, and the peoples around them, are waiting to see how the story ends.

Appendix A: Genealogies

In order to better understand the relationships between various kinds of kin, and in particular the relationships between the people with whom I had contact on a daily basis, I began collecting genealogies from the Manobo in the Elem area in the early 1990s. While my records are hardly exhaustive (they include only 1,219 individuals, living or deceased, versus a current population of about 30,000), they clearly substantiate the great length of time the Manobo have lived in their ancestral territory.

The Manobo only began using surnames in recent generations. They usually employ the name of a prominent ancestor (indicated in bold type for Anggah Kalabaw and Jamin Kapitan). Occasionally, however, they may identify with a more prominent relative of their own direct forebears, as in the case of Adug Nayam.

Kelisong	Kelisong	Kelisong
|	|	|
Kalingutan	Selumay	Selumay
|	|	|
Sengibu	Awen	Awen
|	|	|
Tumundug	Mandalì	Mandalì
|	|	|
Kélê	**Kalabaw**	**Kapitan**
|	|	|
Dimaug	Alun Kalabaw	Eméng Kapitan
|	|	|
Agis	Tektek Kalabaw	Kendung Kapitan
(full brother to Nayam)	|	|
|	Anggah née Kalabaw	Gepi Kapitan
Kasuk Nayam	|	|
|	(children:	Dadù Kapitan
Gunsal Nayam	names not recorded)	|
|		Jamin Kapitan
Adug Nayam		
|		
(children:		
names not recorded)		

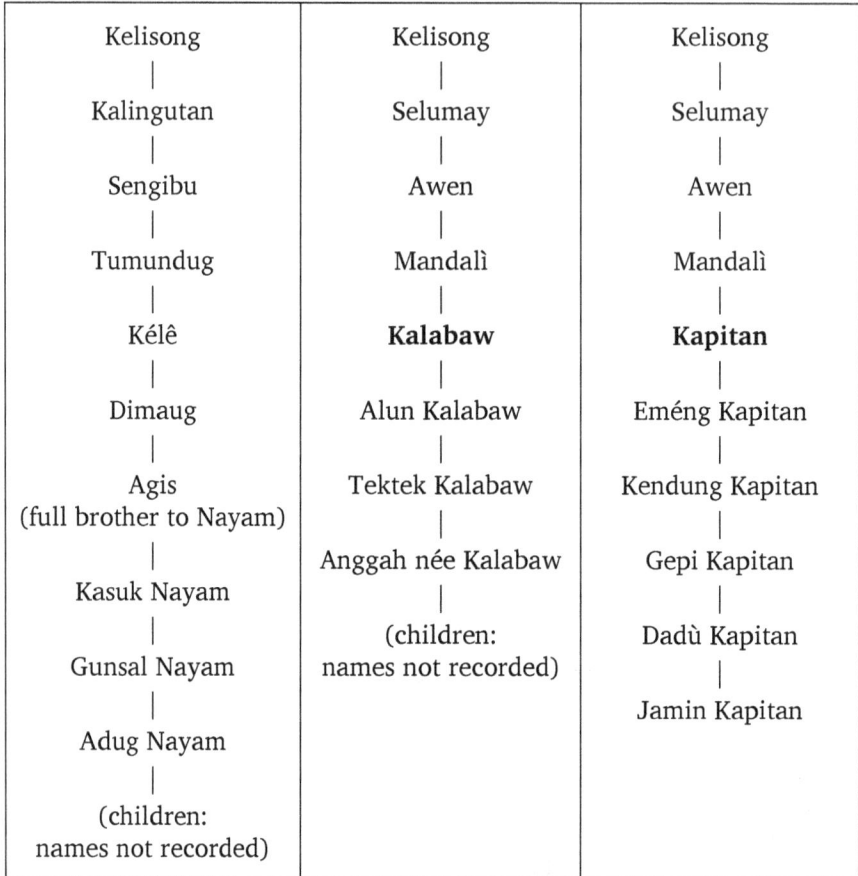

Figure A. Genealogies of three Manobo individuals.

Appendix B: Glossary of Manobo and Scientific Terms

English	Manobo	Scientific[a]
abaca	*kedungon, waka*	*Musa textilis*
basil	*bawing*	*Ocimum basilicum* L.
beggar's tick	*belebek*	*Bidens* sp.
blue-breasted quail	*pugù*	*Coturnix chinensis*
buffalo grass	*lagidit*	*Paspalum conjugatum* Bergius
cassava	*katilà kayu*	*Manihot utilissima (esculenta)* Pohl.
chestnut munia	*maya*	*Lonchura malacca*
Chinese cabbage, Chinese white cabbage, napa cabbage	*petsai*	*Brassica rapa var. pekinensis*
Chinese mustard	*sabì*	*Brassica juncea*
cogon	*elê*	*Imperata cylindrica*
coleto	*tugkeling*	*Sarcops calvus*
cowpea	*putù*	*Vigna sinensis Endl.*

cutworm	*tepelak*	*Spodoptera litura*
deer	*seladeng*	*Cervus (Rusa)* sp.
eggplant	*segutong*	*Solanum melongena* L.
fire ant	*kelitoy*	
foxtail millet	*betem*	*Seratia italica*
goosegrass	*lawil*	*Eleusine indica* (L.) Gaertn.
grain sorghum	*gingoy*	*Sorghum bicolor* L. Moench
greater Asian yam, or possibly Asiatic bitter yam (intoxicating yam)	*bugan*	a wild plant having an edible (and marketable) root, tuber, or corm; probably *Dioscorea alata,* possibly *Dioscorea hispida*
green onion	*lansunà*	*Allium cepa* L.
hornbill (several species)	*kòkò*	
Irish potato	*patatas*	*Solanum tuberosum*
jackfruit	*badak*	*Artocarpus heterophyllus*
Job's tears	*ilah*	*Coix lacryma-jobi*
lantana	*kemahùmahù, kedoo*	*Lantana camara*
lemongrass	*balinggusan*	*Cymbopogon* sp.
lima bean, butter bean	*selawì*	*Phaseolus lunatus* L.
maize, corn	*kelang*	*Zea mays*
mallow family		Malvaceae
mole cricket	*kelool*	*Gryllotalpa africana*
peanut	*lugasing*	*Arachis hypogaea*
pearl millet	*betem*	*Pennisetum glaucum*
Philippine eagle	*banug*	*Pithecophaga jefferyi*
Philippine palm civet	*lekipes*	*Paradoxurus philippinensis* Jourdan, 1837
Philippine tarsier	*emal*	*Tarsius philippensis* Meyer
pig	*babuy*	*Sus celebensis philippensis* Nehring
pigweed	*agum*	*Amaranthus* spp.
rattan	*belagen*	*Calamus* spp.
rice	*palay*	*Oryza sativa*

rice stink bug	*tenangaw*	*Leptocorisa oratorius*
sesame	*lenga*	*Sesamum indicum*
slender-billed crow	*uwak*	*Corvus enca sierramadrensis* Rand and Rabor
squash	*tapasal*	*Cucurbita* sp.
strangler fig	*lakeg*	*Ficus* sp.
sugarcane	*tigdà, tebu*	*Saccharinum officinale*
sweet potato	*katilà*	*Ipomea batatas*
taro	*ludeng*	*Colocasia esculenta*
tilapia	*tilapiya*	*Oreochromis niloticus*
tomato	*kamantis*	*Lycopersicon esculentum* Mill.
toothache plant, paracress	*mekepenù*	a short herbaceous plant having small yellow flowers with a conical central section; probably *Acmella* sp., possibly *Acmella oleracea*
white lauan	*lawaan*	*Shorea contorta* (Vidal) Merrill et Rolfe
white-eared brown dove	*limuken*	*Phapitreron leucotis*
wild betel nut	*kuhan*	*Areca* sp., perhaps *Areca triandra* Roxb. ex Buch.-Ham.
wild fern	*paku*	*Diplazium esculentum (Retz.)* Sw.
wild starch palm (probably fishtail palm)	*basag*	probably *Caryota cumingii* Lodd. ex Mart.
wild yam	*biking*	probably *Dioscorea alata*
woodpecker (unidentified small species)	*kulilit*	
yam, tropical yam	*katilà*	*Dioscorea esculenta*
yautia	*bantanì*	*Yautia xanthosoma*

[a] Bird species were identified from Gonzales and Rees (1988); mammalian species, from Rabor (1986).

Appendix C: Significant Publications on the Cotabato Manobo

Apang, Nida Guil-an. 2001. Transitional literacy among the Cotabato Manobo. *Notes on Literacy* 27(4):19–24.

Errington, Ellen Joyce. 1998. From non-literate to literate practice: The process and effects of introducing a writing system in a cultural community of the Republic of the Philippines. MA thesis. University of Toronto.

Errington, Ross. 1979. A transition network grammar of Cotabato Manobo. *Studies in Philippine Linguistics* 3(2):105–163.

Errington, Ross. 1984. Hortatory mitigation: The case of the camouflaged backbone. *Studies in Philippine Linguistics* 5(1):161–195.

Errington, Ross. 1988. The magic of the Cotabato Manobos. *Studies in Philippine Linguistics* 7(1):153–164.

Fraiser, Douglas M. 1999. In search of a place: Analysis of a land conflict involving the Cotabato Manobo people. SIL Electronic Working Papers 1999–007:1-24. Electronic document, http://www.sil.org/resources/publications/entry/7878. Accessed 3 October 2018.

Lynip, Stephen A. 1988. Culture change among the Cotabato Manobo: Community health education and literacy programming in the milieu of social upheaval. MA thesis, Loma Linda University, CA.

Malone, Susan E., and Dennis L. Malone. 2001. Literacy for development in multilingual contexts: Five characteristics of sustainable programs. *Philippine Journal of Linguistics, Community Development, Literacy and Education* 32(2):11–23.

A more complete bibliography of 83 publications on the Cotabato Manobo people and language can be found on the OLAC Resources website, http://www.language-archives.org/language/mta (accessed 3 October 2018). A complete bibliography on all of the 22 Manobo languages of Mindanao is beyond the scope of this book. SIL linguists have published a total of 215 academic publications on twelve of the Manobo language groups (including thirty papers on Cotabato Manobo). These twelve are Agusan Manobo, Ata Manobo, Binukid, Cotabato Manobo, Dibabawon Manobo, Ilianen Manobo, Kagayanen, Matigsalug Manobo, Obo Manobo, Sarangani Manobo, Tagabawa, and Western Bukidnon Manobo. References to all 215 publications are available on the SIL "Language & Culture Archives" website, https://www.sil.org/resources/archives (accessed 3 October 2018).

References

Abigan, Edmundo R., Jr. 1988a. *Maguindanao*. Las Piñas, Metro Manila, Philippines: M & L Enterprises.

Abigan, Edmundo R., Jr. 1988b. *South Cotabato*. Las Piñas, Metro Manila, Philippines: M & L Enterprises.

Abigan, Edmundo R., Jr. 1988c. *Sultan Kudarat*. Las Piñas, Metro Manila, Philippines: M & L Enterprises.

Adam, F., and B. Rončević. 2003. Social capital: Recent debates and research trends. *Social Science Information* 42:155–183.

Adams, Richard N. 1975. *Energy and structure: Theory of social power*. Austin: University of Texas Press.

Adams, Richard N. 1977. Power in human societies: A synthesis. In Raymond Fogelson and Richard Adams (eds.), *The anthropology of power*, 387–410. New York: Academic Press.

Adams, Richard N. 1988. *The eighth day: Social evolution as the self-organization of energy*. Austin: University of Texas Press.

Allison, Karen J. 1984. *A view from the islands: The Samal of Tawi-tawi*. Dallas, TX: International Museum of Cultures.

Arce, Wilfredo F. 1979. The structural bases of compadre characteristics in a Bikol town. In Mary Racelis Hollnsteiner (ed.), *Society, culture and the Filipino: A textbook of readings in anthropology and sociology*, 108–122. Quezon City: Institute of Philippine Culture, Ateneo de Manila University.

Arce, Wilfredo F., and Necito S. Poblador. 1979. Formal organizations in the Philippines: Motivation, behavior, structure and change. In Mary

Racelis Hollnsteiner (ed.), *Society, culture and the Filipino: A textbook of readings in anthropology and sociology*, 167–178. Quezon City: Institute of Philippine Culture, Ateneo de Manila University.

Berkes, Fikret. 1989a. Cooperation from the perspective of human ecology. In Fikret Berkes (ed.), *Common property resources: Ecology and community-based sustainable development*, 70–88. London: Belhaven.

Berkes, Fikret. 1989b. Multiple-resource cases and integrated development. In Fikret Berkes (ed.), *Common property resources: Ecology and community-based sustainable development*, 237–239. London: Belhaven.

Boserup, Ester. 1965. *The conditions of agricultural growth: The economics of agrarian change under population pressure*. Chicago, IL: Aldine.

Burt, Ronald S. 2002. Bridge decay. *Social Networks* 24:333–363.

Capistrano, Zea Io Ming C. 2015. Manobo activist in Sultan Kudarat feared dead. Accessed 3 October 2018. Electronic document, http://davaotoday.com/main/human-rights/manobo-activist-in-sultan-kudarat-feared-dead/.

Castro, Benny Y. n.d. History of Barangay Keytodac. Unpublished manuscript.

Clemmer, Richard O. 2009. Pristine Aborigines or victims of progress? *Current Anthropology* 50:849–881.

Conklin, Harold C. 1975 [1957]. Hanunóo agriculture: A report on an integral system of shifting cultivation in the Philippines. FAO Forestry Development Paper No. 12. Reprint. Northford, CT: Elliot's Books.

Contreras, Antonio P. 2003. Creating space for local forest management: The case of the Philippines. In David Edmunds and Eva Wollenberg (eds.), *Local forest management: The impacts of devolution policies*, 127–149. London: Earthscan Publications.

De Raedt, Jules. 1991. Similarities and differences in lifestyles in the Central Cordillera of Northern Luzon, Philippines. In A. Terry Rambo and Kathleen Gillogly (eds.), *Profiles in cultural evolution: Papers from a conference in honor of Elman R. Service*. Anthropological Papers 85, 353–372. Ann Arbor: Museum of Anthropology, University of Michigan.

Douglas, Mary. 1970. *Natural symbols: Explorations in cosmology*. New York: Pantheon.

Drucker, Charles Bernard. 1974. Economics and social organization in the Philippine Highlands. Ph.D. dissertation, Department of Anthropology, Stanford University.

Dulce, Leon. 2015. DMCI: Deforestation, mining, coal, and injustice. Accessed 3 October 2018. Electronic document, http://www.rappler.com/move-ph/ispeak/95110-dmci-deforestation-mining-coal-injustice.

Early, John D., and Thomas N. Headland. 1998. *Population dynamics of a Philippine rain forest people: The San Ildefonso Agta*. Gainesville: University Press of Florida.

Eder, James F. 1991. The diversity and cultural evolutionary trajectory of Philippine "Negrito" Populations. In A. Terry Rambo and Kathleen

Gillogly (eds.), *Profiles in cultural evolution: Papers from a conference in honor of Elman R. Service.* Anthropological Papers 85, 247–259. Ann Arbor: Museum of Anthropology, University of Michigan.

Edmunds, David, Eva Wollenberg, Antonio P. Contreras, Liu Dachange, Govind Kelkar, Dev Nathan, Madhu Sarin, and Neera M. Singh. 2003. Introduction. In David Edmunds and Eva Wollenberg (eds.), *Local forest management: The impacts of devolution policies,* 1–19. London: Earthscan.

Elkins, Richard E. 1968. Three models of Western Bukidnon Manobo kinship. *Ethnology* 7(2):171–198.

Fine, Ben. 2000. *Social capital versus social theory: Political economy and social science at the turn of the millennium.* London: Routledge.

Firth, Raymond. 1951. *Elements of social organization.* Boston, MA: Beacon.

Florida Netlink. n.d. Florida State Facts & Figures. Accessed 3 October 2018. Electronic document, http://www.floridanetlink.com/floridafacts.php.

Forestry Department, Food and Agriculture Organization. 2005. Global forest resources assessment: Progress towards sustainable forest management. FAO Forestry Paper 147. Accessed 3 October 2018. Electronic document, http://www.fao.org/docrep/008/a0400e/a0400e00.htm.

Fraiser, Douglas M., and Margaret B. Fraiser. 1991. Cotabato Manobo project. Presented at the Lingenfelter Social Organization Workshop, Bangcud, Bukidnon, Philippines, July 1991. Ms.

Frake, Charles O. 1960. The Eastern Subanon of Mindanao. In G. P. Murdock (ed.), *Social structure in Southeast Asia.* Viking Fund Publication in Anthropology 29, 51–64. Chicago, IL: Quadrangle.

Fried, Morton H. 1975. *The notion of tribe.* Menlo Park, CA: Cummings.

Froese, Deborah. 2015. Peacebuilder allegedly murdered. Accessed 3 October 2018. Electronic document, http://news.mennonitechurch.ca/peacebuilder-allegedly-murdered.

Garvan, John M. 1941. *The Manóbos of Mindanáo.* Memoirs of the National Academy of Sciences, vol. 23, 1st memoir. Presented to the Academy at the Annual Meeting, 1929. Washington, DC: US Govt. Printing Office.

George, T. J. S. 1980. *Revolt in Mindanao: The rise of Islam in Philippine politics.* Oxford: Oxford University Press.

Gonzales, Pedro C., and Colin P. Rees. 1988. *Birds of the Philippines.* Manila: Haribon Foundation for the Conservation of Natural Resources.

Granovetter, Mark. 1973. The strength of weak ties. *American Journal of Sociology* 78:1360–1380.

Gross, Jonathan, and Steve Rayner. 1985. *Measuring culture.* New York: Columbia University Press.

Hardin, Garrett. 1968. The tragedy of the commons. *Science* 162:1243–1248.

Harris, Marvin. 1997. *Culture, people, and nature: An introduction to general anthropology.* New York: Longman.

Harriss, John. 2001. *Depoliticizing development: The World Bank and social capital.* London: Anthem.

Heston, Alan, Robert Summers, and Bettina Aten. 2006. Penn world table Version 6.2. Center for International Comparisons of Production, Income and Prices, University of Pennsylvania. Accessed 5 June 2015. https://pwt.sas.upenn.edu/php_site/pwt62/pwt62_form.php.

Hires, George A., and Thomas N. Headland. 1977. A sketch of Western Bukidnon Manobo farming practices, past and present. *Philippine Quarterly of Culture and Society* 5:65–75.

Hollnsteiner, Mary Racelis. 1979a. Reciprocity as a Filipino value. In Mary Racelis Hollnsteiner (ed.), *Society, culture and the Filipino: A textbook of readings in anthropology and sociology*, 38–43. Quezon City: Institute of Philippine Culture, Ateneo de Manila University.

Hollnsteiner, Mary Racelis. 1979b. Social control, the individual and social change. In Mary Racelis Hollnsteiner (ed.), *Society, culture and the Filipino: A textbook of readings in anthropology and sociology*, 284–286. Quezon City: Institute of Philippine Culture, Ateneo de Manila University.

Hollnsteiner, Mary Racelis, ed. 1979. *Society, culture and the Filipino: A textbook of readings in anthropology and sociology.* Quezon City: Institute of Philippine Culture, Ateneo de Manila University.

Hudson, A. B. 1972. Padju Epat: *The Ma'anyan of Indonesian Borneo.* New York: Holt, Rinehart and Winston.

Human Rights Watch. 1996. The Philippines: Human rights and forest management in the 1990s. Human Rights Watch 8(3C). Accessed 3 October 2018. http://hrw.org/reports/1996/Philippi.htm.

Hunt, Robert C., and Antonio Gilman. 1998. Preface. In Robert C. Hunt and Antonio Gilman (eds.), *Property in economic context.* Society for Economic Anthropology Monograph Series, 14, vii–ix. New York: University Press of America.

Hutterer, Karl L. 1991. Losing track of the tribes: Evolutionary sequences in Southeast Asia. In A. Terry Rambo and Kathleen Gillogly (eds.), *Profiles in cultural evolution: Papers from a conference in honor of Elman R. Service.* Anthropological Papers 85, 219–245. Ann Arbor: Museum of Anthropology, University of Michigan.

Jocano, F. Landa. 1969. *The traditional world of Malitbog.* Quezon City: University of the Philippines.

Jocano, F. Landa. 1997. Filipino value system: A cultural definition. *Anthropology of the Filipino People* 4. Metro Manila: PUNLAD Research House.

Jocano, F. Landa. 1998a. Filipino indigenous ethnic communities: Patterns, variations, and typologies. *Anthropology of the Filipino People* 2. Metro Manila: PUNLAD Research House.

Jocano, F. Landa. 1998b. Filipino social organization: Traditional kinship and family organization. *Anthropology of the Filipino People* 3. Metro Manila: PUNLAD Research House.

Kapferer, Bruce. 1997. Millenarian movements. In Thomas Barfield (ed.), *The dictionary of anthropology,* 324–325. Malden, MA: Blackwell.

Keesing, Roger M. 1975. *Kin groups and social structure.* Fort Worth, TX: Holt, Rinehart and Winston.

Kerr, Harland. 1988a. Cotabato Manobo ethnography. *Studies in Philippine linguistics* 7(1):125–151.

Kerr, Harland. 1988b. Cotabato Manobo grammar. *Studies in Philippine linguistics* 7(1):1–123.

Kracht, Benjamin R. 1992. The Kiowa ghost dance, 1894–1916: An unheralded revitalization movement. *Ethnohistory* 39(4):452–477.

Krebs, Valdis E. n.d. Managing the connected organization. Accessed 3 October 2018. http://www.orgnet.com/MCO.html.

Lansing, J. Stephen, and Therese A. de Vet. 1999. Nias revisited: Head-hunting, chieftainship, and alliance. In Lorraine V. Aragon and Susan D. Russell (eds.), *Structuralism's transformations: Order and revision in Indonesian and Malaysian societies,* 69–91. Tempe, AZ: Program for Southeast Asian Studies, Arizona State University.

Lee, Richard Borshay. 1979. *The !Kung San: Men, women and work in a foraging society.* Cambridge, NY: Cambridge University Press.

Lewis, M. Paul, Gary F. Simons, and Charles D. Fennig, eds. 2015a. Manobo: Cotabato. *Ethnologue: Languages of the world.* 18th edition. Dallas, TX: SIL International. Accessed 24 July 2015. http://www.ethnologue.com/language/mta.

Lewis, M. Paul, Gary F. Simons, and Charles D. Fennig, eds. 2015b. Philippines. *Ethnologue: Languages of the world.* 18th edition. Dallas: SIL International. Accessed 24 July 2015. http://www.ethnologue.com/country/PH.

Lingenfelter, Sherwood G. 1990. Introduction. In Sherwood G. Lingenfelter (ed.), *Social organization of Sabah societies,* 1–12. Kota Kinabalu, Sabah, Malaysia: Department of Sabah Museum and State Archives.

Lozano, Joey R. B. 1996. "Corporate trees" conquer lumads. Accessed 22 November 2003. http://humanrights.uchicago.edu/joeylozano/joey05.html.

Lynch, Frank. 1979a. Big and little people: Social class in the rural Philippines. In Mary Racelis Hollnsteiner (ed.), *Society, culture and the Filipino: A textbook of readings in anthropology and sociology,* 44–48. Quezon City: Institute of Philippine Culture, Ateneo de Manila University.

Lynch, Frank. 1979b. Perspectives on Filipino clannishness. In Mary Racelis Hollnsteiner (ed.), *Society, culture and the Filipino: A textbook of readings in anthropology and sociology,* 103–107. Quezon City: Institute of Philippine Culture, Ateneo de Manila University.

Man, W. K. Che. 1990. *Muslim separatism: The Moros of southern Philippines and the Malays of southern Thailand.* Oxford: Oxford University Press.

Manuel, E. Arsenio. 1973. *Manuvu' social organization.* Quezon City: Community Development Research Council, University of the Philippines.

Marshall, Lorna. 1976. Sharing, talking, and giving: Relief of social tensions among the !Kung. In Richard B. Lee and Irven DeVore (eds.), *Kalahari hunter-gatherers*, 349–371. Cambridge, MA: Harvard University Press.

Martin, John H., Warren H. Leonard, and David L. Stamp. 1976. *Principles of field crop production.* New York: Macmillan.

Mayers, Marvin K. 1980. *A look at Filipino life styles.* International Museum of Cultures Publication, 8. Dallas: International Museum of Cultures.

Murdock, George Peter. 1965. *Social structure.* New York: Free Press.

National Mapping and Resource Information Center. 1990[1975]. Buluan. Second edition. Makati, Philippines: NAMRIA.

Oliva, Roberto. 1998. Sustainable forest management through multisectoral forest protection committees: Philippine experience. Accessed 14 November 2003. http://srdis.ciesin.columbia.edu/cases/philippines-011.html.

Ostrom, Elinor. 1990. *Governing the commons: The evolution of institutions for collective action.* Cambridge, UK: Cambridge University Press.

PAFID. n.d.a. Present land use map of Tribal Community of Esperanza Association. Quezon City, Philippines: PAFID.

PAFID. n.d.b. Tribal Community of Lebak Association (TCLA) Present land use map. Quezon City, Philippines: PAFID.

Panya, Opart. 1991. Social ecology of Thai peasant society: The impact of larger and external social relations (1850–1950). In A. Terry Rambo and Kathleen Gillogly (eds.), *Profiles in cultural evolution: Papers from a conference in honor of Elman R. Service.* Anthropological Papers 85, 405–428. Ann Arbor: Museum of Anthropology, University of Michigan.

Poggie, John J. 1995. Food resource periodicity and cooperation values: A cross-cultural consideration. *Cross-cultural Research* 29(3):276–296.

Population Reference Bureau. 2015. 2014 World population data sheet. Accessed 3 October 2018. http://www.prb.org/pdf14/2014-world-population-data-sheet_eng.pdf.

Pospisil, Leopold J. 1978. *The Kapauku Papuans of West New Guinea.* Second edition. New York, NY: Holt, Rinehart and Winston.

Putnam, Robert. 1993. *Making democracy work: Civic traditions in modern Italy.* Princeton, NJ: Princeton University Press.

Rabor, Dioscoro S. 1986. *Guide to Philippine flora and fauna. Vol. 11: Birds, mammals.* Quezon City: Natural Resources Management Center, Ministry of Natural Resources, and University of the Philippines.

Rachman, Ali M. A. 1991. Social integration and energy utilization: An analysis of the *Kubu suku terasing* of Indonesia and the *temuan orang asli* of Malaysia. In A. Terry Rambo and Kathleen Gillogly (eds.), *Profiles in cultural evolution: Papers from a conference in honor of Elman R. Service.* Anthropological Papers 85, 311–331. Ann Arbor: Museum of Anthropology, University of Michigan.

Rambo, A. Terry. 1991a. Energy and the evolution of culture: A reassessment of White's Law. In A. Terry Rambo and Kathleen Gillogly (eds.), *Profiles in cultural evolution: Papers from a conference in honor of Elman R. Service.* Anthropological Papers 85, 291–310. Ann Arbor: Museum of Anthropology, University of Michigan.

Rambo, A. Terry. 1991b. The study of cultural evolution. In A. Terry Rambo and Kathleen Gillogly (eds.), *Profiles in cultural evolution: Papers from a conference in honor of Elman R. Service.* Anthropological Papers 85, 23–109. Ann Arbor: Museum of Anthropology, University of Michigan.

Sajise, Percy E. 1991. Ethnic groups in transition and some of their impacts on the hinterland environments of Southeast Asia: Are there lessons to be learned? In A. Terry Rambo and Kathleen Gillogly (eds.), *Profiles in cultural evolution: Papers from a conference in honor of Elman R. Service.* Anthropological Papers 85, 429–450. Ann Arbor: Museum of Anthropology, University of Michigan.

Sanchez, Pedro A. 1976. *Properties and management of soils in the tropics.* New York, NY: Wiley.

Schlegel, Stuart A. 1970. *Tiruray justice: Traditional Tiruray law and morality.* Berkeley: University of California Press.

Schlegel, Stuart A. 1979. *Tiruray subsistence: From shifting cultivation to plow agriculture.* Quezon City: Ateneo de Manila University Press.

Scott, John. 2000. *Social network analysis: A handbook.* Second edition. Thousand Oaks, CA: Sage.

Service, Elman R. 1968. The prime-mover of cultural evolution. *Southwestern Journal of Anthropology* 24:396–409.

Service, Elman R. 1993. Political power and the origin of social complexity. In John S. Henderson and Patricia J. Netherly (eds.), *Configurations of power: Holistic anthropology in theory and practice,* 112–134. Ithaca, NY: Cornell University Press.

Singelis, Theodore M., Harry C. Triandis, Dharm P. S. Bhawuk, and Michele J. Gelfand. 1995. Horizontal and vertical dimensions of individualism and collectivism: A theoretical and measurement refinement. *Cross-cultural Research* 29(3):240–275.

Small, D., and N. B. Tannenbaum. 1999a. Archaeology of the interface: A brief overview. In David B. Small and Nicola Tannenbaum (eds.), *At the interface: The household and beyond.* Monographs in Economic Anthropology 15, 173. New York, NY: University Press of America.

Small, D., and N. B. Tannenbaum. 1999b. Interfaces and the organization of communities: A brief overview. In David B. Small and Nicola Tannenbaum (eds.), *At the interface: The household and beyond.* Monographs in Economic Anthropology 15, 75–76. New Yor, NY: University Press of America.

Sohmer, S. H. 1992. How many trees does a forest make? In Thomas N. Headland and Doris E. Blood (eds.), *What place for hunter-gatherers in millennium three?*, 47–58. Dallas, TX: SIL International and International Museum of Cultures.

Spradley, James P., and David W. McCurdy. 1980. *Anthropology: The cultural perspective.* New York, NY: Wiley.

Szanton, M. Cristina Blanc. 1979. Personalized exchange: The "suki" relationship. In Mary Racelis Hollnsteiner (ed.), *Society, culture and the Filipino: A textbook of readings in anthropology and sociology*, 62–69. Quezon City: Institute of Philippine Culture, Ateneo de Manila University.

Thompson, Michael, Richard Ellis, and Aaron Wildavsky. 1980. *Cultural theory.* Boulder: Westview Press.

World Bank. 2002a. Social capital and civil society. Accessed 4 June 2004. http://www.worldbank.org/poverty/scapital/sources/civil2.htm.

World Bank. 2002b. Social capital and community. Accessed 4 June 2004. http://www.worldbank.org/poverty/scapital/sources/comm1.htm.

World Bank. 2002c. Social capital and firms. Accessed 4 June 2004. http://www.worldbank.org/poverty/scapital/sources/firm1.htm.

Yen, D. E., and Hermes Gutierrez. 1976. The ethnobotany of the Tasaday: I. The useful plants. In Douglas E. Yen and John Nance (eds.), *Further studies on the Tasaday*, 97–136. Makati, Philippines: PANAMIN.

Yengoyan, Aram A. 1991. Evolutionary theory in ethnological perspectives. In A. Terry Rambo and Kathleen Gillogly (eds.), *Profiles in cultural evolution: Papers from a conference in honor of Elman R. Service.* Anthropological Papers 85, 3–21. Ann Arbor: Museum of Anthropology, University of Michigan.

Youngblood-Coleman, Denise, ed. n.d. Philippines: Country review. Accessed 3 October 2018. http://www.countrywatch.com/Intelligence/CountryReviews?CountryId = 137.

Index

SIL International® Publications
Publications in Ethnography Series
ISSN 0-0895-9897

47. **Bajju Christian conversion in the Middle Belt of Nigeria,** by Carol V. McKinney, 2019, 202 pp., ISBN 978-1-55671-398-9.

46. **Baranzan's people: An ethnohistory of the Bajju of the Middle Belt of Nigeria,** by Carol V. McKinney, 2019, 238 pp., ISBN 978-1-55671-399-6.

45. **Acclimated to Africa: Cultural competence for Westerners,** by Debbi DiGennaro, 2017, 163 pp., ISBN 978-1-55671-386-6.

44. **The heart of the matter: Seeking the center in Maya-Mam language and culture,** by Wesley M. Collins, 2015, 205 pp., ISBN 978-1-55671-375-0.

43. **African friends and money matters.** Second edition, by David E. Maranz, 2015, 293 pp., ISBN 978-1-55671-277-7.

42. **Ensnared by AIDS: Cultural contexts of HIV and AIDS in Nepal,** by David K. Beine, 2014, 357 pp., ISBN 978-1-55671-350-7.

41. **The Norsk Høstfest: A celebration of ethnic food and ethnic identity,** by Paul Thomas Emch, 2011, 121 pp., ISBN 978-1-55671-265-4.

40. **Our company increases apace: History, language, and social identity in early colonial Andover,** Massachusetts, by Elinor Abbot, 2007, 279 pp., ISBN 978-1-55671-169-5.

39. **What place for hunters-gatherers in millennium three?** by Thomas N. Headland and Doris E. Blood, eds. 2002, 130 pp., ISBN 978-1-55671-132-9.

38. **A tale of Pudicho's people,** by Richard Montag. 2002, 181 pp., ISBN 978-1-55671-131-2.

SIL International® Publications
7500 W. Camp Wisdom Road
Dallas, Texas 75236-5629 USA

General inquiry: publications_intl@sil.org
Pending order inquiry: sales@sil.org
publications.sil.org

About the Author

Douglas M. Fraiser earned a BS in agronomy from Texas A&M University, an MS in agronomy from the University of Florida, and a PhD in interdisciplinary ecology (concentration: anthropology) from the University of Florida. He and his wife, Meg, lived and worked with the Manobo people of the Philippines from 1983 through 2002. Since then they have worked in Malaysia and Thailand.

Doug currently teaches at Payap University in Chiang Mai, Thailand and coordinates SIL International's cultural research in Mainland Southeast Asia. He also serves on the adjunct faculty of the University of North Dakota and has been a senior anthropology consultant with SIL International since 2012. His research interests include

- social, economic, and political organization
- farming systems
- agroforestry and deforestation
- land tenure and land use
- worldview
- religious movements, and
- culture change.

Selected publications

2017. Planting prosperity, cultivating community: Language and magic in the dooryard gardens of Northern Thailand. In ฐิติ ฐิติจำเริญพร [Thiti Thitichamroenphorn] (ed.), *Proceedings of the Payap University Research Symposium*, Chiang Mai, Thailand, 10 February 2017, 564–577. Payap University: Research and Academic Service Affairs.

2013. The participatory approach: Illustrations from experience. *ECHO Asia Notes* 18:2–5.

2001. Land conflict of the Cotabato Manobo people. *Philippine Studies* 49:215–235.

1997. Literacy and the economic context: The cultural dimension of development. *INNOTECH Journal* 21.2, 1–11.

1997. *Ini sa ukit ta eg-ipat tanà ta kayu* [This is how we use trees to care for our land]. Manila, Philippines: Summer Institute of Linguistics.

1993. *Ini sa ukit ta egbael basakan* [This is how we make rice paddies]. Manila, Philippines: Summer Institute of Linguistics.

1992. *Ini sa ukit ta eghagtay sedà* [This is how we raise fish]. Lebak, Sultan Kudarat, Philippines: Association of Manobo Bible Churches.

Academic website

https://www.sil.org/biography/doug-fraiser

www.ingramcontent.com/pod-product-compliance
Lightning Source LLC
Chambersburg PA
CBHW062031270326
41929CB00014B/2393